GOD'S KINGDOM AND
THE UTOPIAN ERROR

GOD'S KINGDOM
AND THE
UTOPIAN
ERROR

Discerning the Biblical Kingdom of God from Its Political Counterfeits

Peter P. J. Beyerhaus

CROSSWAY BOOKS • WHEATON, ILLINOIS
A DIVISION OF GOOD NEWS PUBLISHERS

First printing, 1992

Printed in the United States of America

Library of Congress Cataloging-in-Publication Data
Beyerhaus, Peter P. J.
   God's Kingdom and the utopian error : discerning the biblical
kingdom of God from its political counterfeits / Peter P. J. Beyerhaus.
      p.   cm.
   Includes bibliographical references and index.
    1. Kingdom of God. 2. Utopias—Religious aspects. 3.
Missions. 4. Evangelistic work. 5. Evangelicalism.
BT94.B48 1992   231.7'2—dc20   91-31086
ISBN 0-89107-651-4

00	99	98	97	96	95	94	93	92
15	14	13	12	11	10	9	8	7	6	5	4	3	2	1

TABLE OF

CONTENTS

PREFACE

This book follows up on a series of publications in the early seventies in which I attempted to introduce to an English-speaking audience my assessment of the fundamental crisis into which the world missionary movement had run because of the deep erosion of its biblical foundations. Under the headings *Missions—Which Way?* (1972), *Shaken Foundations* (1973), and *Bangkok '73—Beginning or End of World Mission?* (1974),[1] I focused on the dramatic developments within ecumenical missiology since the integration of the former International Missionary Council into the World Council of Churches in New Delhi 1961, as well as the climactic events of the Fourth Assembly at Uppsala 1968 and the 8th World Missionary Conference in Thailand. These events caused a growing uneasiness within the evangelical constituency, both within the conciliar movement and without, and soon led to the apologetic reaction voiced in the famous Declarations of Wheaton in 1966 and Frankfurt in 1970.

Although my critical account of the "experiment in group dynamics," to which my 315 fellow participants and I were exposed in Bangkok, has until now remained my last book in English, my personal concern in the two wings of the world missionary movement has by no means receded. On the contrary, I have remained an interested student of all ecumenical conferences with missiological significance since then, attending most of them as a press observer and publishing analyses of them in German books and articles. Since the frustrating experience at Bangkok my constructive involvement, however, has shifted to the evangelical movement for world evangelization, starting with the historical congress in Lausanne 1974. I have participated, normally as a speaker, in most of its consultations and conferences since then, including its recent second world congress in Manila (1989).

The very fact that both in 1980 and in 1989 the two wings of the international missionary movement called for separate world conferences in their own sponsorship demonstrates that the missiological polarization caused by the contrasting courses taken at Bangkok in 1973 and Lausanne in 1974 has by no means been resolved, in spite of several attempts made by certain representatives on both sides to do so. In fact, the Open Letter, in which 160 participants "with evangelical concerns" at San Antonio pleaded with the participants of the Manila Congress to support their proposal that the next meeting be a joint meeting, received a cool reaction from the Lausanne Executive Committee because of the deep theological rift between the two camps.

What actually is the heart of the matter in the evangelical-ecumenical conflict can and has been discussed. There are those evangelicals who suggest that it is the imbalance between social action and evangelism on the side of the conciliar movement which has distorted the biblical view of the missionary task. Adjusting the balance would then be the solution to the problem. This is in fact what representatives of the "radical evangelicals"—i.e., the main spokesmen for an agreement between the two movements—are suggesting. If evangelicals would learn from their ecumenical colleagues and squarely face the sociopolitical challenges of the Third World, and if, on the other hand, ecumenicals would show more readiness to respond to the spiritual needs of the vast number of unreached people groups, in their opinion a merger would be feasible.

There is, indeed, a grain of truth in this consideration. But its weakness is that this is a rather pragmatic approach which does not penetrate deeply enough into the theological foundations. The fact that evangelicals are more eager to take the gospel to the poor of

the non-Christian world, while the ecumenicals are more concerned with changing the unjust structures of society that cause
their poverty is, in the final analysis, grounded in a deep cleavage
in the understanding of God's plan of redemption. Both sides might
agree, in principle, that God's ultimate purpose is the total salvation of mankind, when both spiritual and physical, individual and
corporate needs are removed. Moreover, both can agree that the
state where this happy situation has been reached can be called in
biblical terminology the *Kingdom of God*. In their efforts to fulfill
their ultimate purpose, Christian missions have in fact always been
inspired by this divine aim as set forth both by the OT prophets and
by the three Synoptic evangelists, based upon Jesus' own preaching.
But the tragedy of the modern international movement was caused
by the fact that the Kingdom became a blurred concept under the
influence of theological liberalism and the Social Gospel as well as
humanist ideologies, but partly also due to different millennial theories. In its most radical distortion it was reduced to a synonym for
whatever ideal state for which people in their various philosophies
of history were hoping.

But there are several degrees of confusion which all are caused
by a basic lack of eschatological precision, or—to use a term from
that continental school of thought in which my theology is rooted—
in a failing awareness of biblical "*Heilsgeschichte*"—i.e., salvation
history. For everything depends on its (i.e., salvation history's) crucial distinctions between the different stages in which the divine
oikonomia, the redemptive economy of God, is unfolded in his
sovereign dealings with his world until its final destination is
reached and all creation becomes a mirror of his glory. To miss this
grand purpose and to become negligent about the stages leading to
it not only introduces theoretical errors, but its realistic consequence is to change the *Kingdom of Heaven*, as promised and given
to God's sons and daughters, into a *Kingdom on Earth* which is to
be constructed solely by the autonomous efforts of man himself.

According to my observations as recorded in this series of
studies, this is what has happened to the Ecumenical Movement in
its development of a new type of missionary vision. It is for that rea-

son I am so passionately concerned that the evangelical wing of the international missionary movement should remain faithful to its biblical orientation. Evangelicals must shun any compromise with ideological counterfeits, even if such proposals are made to them in the name of an alleged "Kingdom Theology" which, by substituting a so-called "Jesus language" for "Pauline language," in fact inverts the internal process of biblical theology from the prophets via the Gospels to the epistles. For by doing thus, such a view misses the decisive point in scriptural salvation history that all promises of God are fulfilled in Christ (2 Cor 1:20) in whose communion, the Church, we are accepted into the Kingdom in its present stage of realization.

This plea to be mindful of God's sovereign economy in establishing his Kingdom is the golden thread which runs through this collection of essays and lectures. The reader will notice that they were prepared at various occasions within a period of sixteen years between the first and second congresses of the Lausanne Movement for World Evangelization. Although the chapters are different in style, and sometimes contain reiterations of arguments set out in earlier places, I have chosen to limit my updating to a minimum in order to retain the original pointed contextuality. I trust that in spite of this, my readers will recognize an internal consistency that renders this publication as a homogeneous theological thrust. My biblical quotations are generally from the *Revised Standard Version*.

Finally, I want to acknowledge the invaluable help of the two editors of this book, Dr. Robert E. L. Rodgers of Bangor, North Ireland, and Dr. John S. Feinberg, of Trinity Evangelical Divinity School, Deerfield, Illinois. They have brushed up my English and occasionally—without injuring the substance of my views—also suggested some theological modifications in order to ensure reception in an ecclesiastical setting shaped by different traditional lines of evangelical thought. I am particularly thankful for these concerns, for I wanted to produce a book not only for the expert in the field but also for the intelligent layman who wishes to be informed about the fundamental issues of the Church's mission and ecumenical thinking today.

THE KINGDOM VISION IN EVANGELICAL ESCHATOLOGY

PART I: THE COMING KING— AN EVANGELICAL FUNDAMENTAL

The theme of the 2nd International Congress for World Evangelization of the Lausanne Movement ("Proclaim Christ *until He comes*!") was noteworthy for reemphasizing a scriptural concern which always has been important for a truly evangelical understanding of missions: its clear orientation towards the second coming of our Lord.

When Arthur T. Pierson in 1886 in his famous address about "The Bible and Prophecy" to D. L. Moody's Mt. Hermon Summer School coined the famous watchword for the Student Volunteer Movement—"The Evangelization of the World in This Generation," he did so from his premillennial conviction that the evangelization of all the nations on earth was the condition laid down by Jesus himself in his eschatological speech on the Mt. of Olives for his future coming in glory. As Dana Robert remarks, Pierson and those whom he inspired to engage in a great venture to evangelize the world by the dawn of the twentieth century believed that the "sooner the entire world heard the good news of the Gospel, the sooner Jesus Christ would return to usher in the millennium. This millennial hope fueled Pierson's passion for systematic world-evangelization."[1] The eschatological hope implied in this persuasion was very realistic. Pierson and the majority within the early SVM really hoped that the task they were shouldering "could be completed in their lifetime and that they would participate in the second coming of Jesus Christ." This hope was still awake amongst the founding fathers of the International Missionary Movement in 1910. At the end of the famous Edinburgh Conference John Mott, its chairman, in his closing speech dared to claim the possibility that "before many of us taste death we shall see the Kingdom of God come with power."[2]

The Ecumenical Mission Movement begun at Edinburgh and organized in the International Missionary Council was, however, not able to maintain this eschatological motivation. Already Gustav Warneck, the German founder of the science of missiology, very early had criticized the "Anglo-Saxon eschatological optimism" seemingly contained in the SVM's watchword and the "superficial" perception of the missionary task derived from it.[3] Later on, during the 1920s and 1930s, the IMC fell more and more under the influence of modern crosscurrents in theology that stressed the inner-worldly aspects of the Christian gospel and mission, especially the ecclesial and social ones.

The Kingdom of God was still a guiding theme in missionary thinking, but the main stress was laid on the idea of its evolution within history. This caused great concern, particularly within missionary circles in Germany, a concern which found its public expression in a separate declaration given by the German delegation in critical evaluation of the findings of the Madras Meeting in 1938.[4] They pronounced that they were "bound by conscience to point to some vital points of the Gospel, which must be emphasized in contrast with certain passages in the reports of some sections." Over against an inner-worldly interpretation of the Kingdom, they stressed that the Kingdom will be consummated through a creative act of God in the final establishment of a New Heaven and a New

Earth. "We are convinced that only this eschatological attitude can prevent the Church from becoming secularized."[5]

This eschatological concern had arisen amongst German missiological thinkers under the influence of a theological current—drawing especially from the pietistic tradition in Württemberg—which placed the evangelistic task of the Church within the framework of salvation history. Here mission was understood as the overriding task of the Church during the interim period between Christ's first and second comings. This view was expounded emphatically by Karl Hartenstein and Walter Freytag, who found theological support for their concern in the writings of Tübingen dogmatician Karl Heim and Basel NT exegete Oscar Cullmann. Hartenstein and Freytag for the rest of their lives made it their main concern to remind the ecumenical missionary movement about this salvation-historical dimension. For a time (between the IMC's Willingen Meeting in 1952 and the WCC's Assembly at Evanston in 1954) it appeared that their concern had been attended to, but eventually their thrust was completely discarded by the dominating theology of missions in the conciliar movement. This became obvious at the WCC's 4th Assembly at Uppsala 1968[6] and its 8th World Missionary Conference at Bangkok 1973.[7] Both meetings signaled the adoption of views that spelled out mission in categories of humanization, sociopolitical liberation, and dialogue with other religions. In the conciliar movement the "coming world community" virtually had replaced the Kingdom of God as the ultimate vision in mission.

Where German missiology had failed to stem the tide—and finally in the majority of its own representatives even succumbed to it, the newly invigorated evangelical movement raised the eschatological banner again. According to Denton Lotz, it was "in the 1960's that the watchword and the idea of world-evangelization (in this generation) inherent in it took on new lights among leaders of faith missions and evangelical groups."[8] Conservative groups such as the Inter-Varsity Christian Fellowship and the Evangelical Foreign Missions Association in the United States voiced again the battle cry of their grandfathers. For most of them this was not only the voluntaristic proclamation of a gigantic task, but rather a reassertion of the premillennial hope which A. Pierson and his companions once had attached to it.

It is noteworthy that in all important affirmations which evangelicals have publicized in recent decades, the eschatological keynote is sounded highly. This applies to the Wheaton Declaration of 1966,[9] the Frankfurt Declaration of 1970,[10] the Report about the Evangelical Roman-Catholic Dialogue on Mission (ERCDOM) in 1984[11] and, of course, the Lausanne Covenant of 1974.[12] The last paragraph from Lausanne (15) reads:

> We believe that Jesus Christ will return personally and visibly, in power and glory, to consummate his salvation and his judgement. This promise of his coming is a further spur to our evangelism, for we remember his words that the Gospel must first be preached to all nations. We believe that the interim period between Christ's ascension and return is to be filled with the mission of the people of God, who have no liberty to stop before the end. . . .

This is a very clear adoption of the salvation-historical understanding of missions and a well-deserved vindication of the once-abortive attempts of German missiologists such as Walter Freytag to get international recognition for their biblical plea to conceive "mission in view of the end."[13] I regard it as of utmost importance for the Lausanne Movement to remain faithful to this evangelical rediscovery of eschatology. We should not allow the confession of Christ's return to appear just as a decoration, a piece of high-sounding rhetoric, but rather make it the focus of our total conception of Christ's mandate for world evangelization.

PART II: BIBLICAL CONCERNS IN EVANGELICAL ESCHATOLOGY

The decisive reason evangelicals are so keen in making eschatological expectation a pillar of their doctrinal thinking is the fact that they find in the Bible that God's redemptive action in Jesus Christ has a history of which all three tenses—past, present and future—are essential. This history is closely connected with the way in which God in Jesus Christ fulfils the biblical prophecy of the coming of his Kingdom.

Unlike the Jewish expectation at the time of Jesus, God did not establish his messianic reign on earth by one single intervention, but rather by a sequence of stages of which the first two have already taken place. The third one, however, is still postponed. The first decisive Kingdom event was *the incarnation of God's Son in the person of Jesus Christ*, who revealed the gracious will of the Father and accomplished the work of atonement. The second Kingdom event was *Christ's ascension to sit at the right hand of the Father*, where he invisibly exercises his majestic rule over heaven and earth, directing the course of history in such a way that all peoples on earth progressively are being faced with his salvific message and his royal claim. The third yet future stage is *Christ's return, by which he will establish God's Kingdom visibly in power and glory*, thereby finally abolishing every hostile force that still counteracts his holy will and questions the salvation which he has accomplished at his cross.

Evangelical eschatology is clearly opposed to all types of liberal eschatology, for it in various ways and categories tries to eliminate the transcendental reality of this future stage and puts it at the present disposal of man by giving it an existential, mystical, ethical, evolutionary or political interpretation.

Evangelicals, true enough, are divided amongst themselves with regard to whether and how the ultimate reign of God after the creation of a New Heaven and a New Earth will be preceded by a millennium, a rule of Christ which pertains still to this present although greatly transformed earth. Evangelicals who expect a millennial reign of Christ also debate the exact sequence of such a future intervention of Christ. This is obviously the reason comprehensive meetings such as the Lausanne Congresses that are set up to manifest evangelical unity are rather hesitant to give too close considerations to eschatological issues. But I am convinced that we cannot afford to exercise such abstention if we really are looking for biblical guidance in our present missionary task. And I am equally convinced that we need not dodge the issue, because from a higher perspective the particular concerns expressed in the three basic evangelical millennial positions (including the amillennial view) could satisfactorily become resolved. In fact, a recent investigation made by David Hesselgrave[14] has shown that the crucial evangelical concerns with regard to an eschatological understanding of missions could be maintained from each of the three positions if their proponents would allow their views to be modified in the light of the legitimate points of view of the others.

The *amillennial* concern to be heeded is to avoid an understanding of Christ's dominion over the present world which imagines it fancifully in the likeness of one of the historical human empires, making Christ far too small. The *premillennial* concern to be heeded is the prophetic prediction that the present world will never yield completely to messianic conditions until the demonic rebellion still working in this aeon will be dealt with by the dramatic encounter between Christ and Antichrist. The *postmillennial* concern which should not be ignored is that Christians should not become paralyzed by a dualistic pessimism with regard to possible improvements of earthly conditions under the leavening influence of the Holy Spirit sent by the exalted Christ. We are rightfully warned against exercising irresponsible abstinence from sociopolitical involvement.

The most important point, however, which must never be lost sight of by an evangelical who views missions in an eschatological perspective is that the Kingdom in power and glory can and will only be set up by Jesus Christ himself when he returns in his transfigured body, surrounded by all his heavenly host of angels and saints. This deeply desired event will not take place before all people on earth will have heard the testimony of the Kingdom from the mouth of messengers who preach the gospel of Jesus Christ to them (Matt 24:14; Mark 13:10; Acts 1:8). This gives, as Oscar Cullmann has pointed out so convincingly, decisive meaning to the present salvation-historical period between Christ's first and second comings, and it also persuasively explains the so-called "delay of the *parousia*." This temporal interval is needed to accomplish the Great Commission of the Risen One to evangelize and disciple all nations on the inhabited earth.[15]

Cullmann[16] and all theologians sympathizing with his thrust rightly point out that this interim period is characterized by the polar tension between the "already" and the "not yet"—*viz.*, the "only then." Christian missions receive their strength from the spiritual dynamite which has been released *already* by the finished work of Christ at the cross and his resurrection as the firstborn amongst many brethren. This is experienced in the power to untie people from the bonds of a guilty conscience before a holy God, slavery to sin, and bondage to Satan. It is socially manifested in the eschatological community of Christ's Church. It permeates human society in general by inspiring believers and even unregenerated people by the precepts of God's Kingdom as set forth in the Sermon on the Mount, thus laying a foundation for at least a provisional new order marked by justice, social concern and peace.

At the same time a truly evangelical missiology is aware of the eschatological "*not yet*" in our present interim period. The gospel is being preached in a world whose nature and history is still deeply marked by the consequences of the Fall. It is a world in which Satan as its prince still exercises power over all those who have not accepted the redemptive love of God in Jesus Christ. In fact, Jesus and the apostles realistically described the progress of the gospel in the non-Christian world as an ongoing war between two opposing hosts of spiritual forces, heading for the final clash between their heads—Christ and Antichrist. Hence, the progress of Christ's Kingdom on earth is visible only partly and in signs, seemingly without guarantee of permanent duration. Christianity is tempted to disobedience and unbelief by seductive forces, and it is threatened by apostasy which finally will be the condition of its majority (Matt 24:10-13). Only when Christ holds judgment at his second coming will his true followers be revealed and glorified, and at that time there will be separation between the Kingdom of God and the place of the wicked ones condemned to eternal punishment.

This terrible possibility which evangelicals tremblingly maintain in all its reality constitutes a powerful negative reason for urgent world evangelization. Such thinking has inflamed and still does inflame many evangelical Christians with a burning passion to rescue human souls from eternal perdition. When Hudson Taylor in 1894 challenged the SVM at Detroit to offer their lives for mission service in China, he voiced the following touching appeal:

> The Gospel must be preached to those people in very short time, because they walk at the path of death. Every day, every day, oh how they sweep over! There is a great Niagara of souls passing into the dark in China. . . . One million a month in China are dying without God.[17]

These are the main tenets of a Kingdom-centered eschatology which evangelicals have realized to be pertinent to the understanding of Christian missions, both with regard to motivation and conditions. Now we shall point out how these eschatological tenets indeed are seen in their relevance for their practice of world evangelization.

PART III: THE MISSIONARY RELEVANCE OF THE KINGDOM VISION (ESCHATOLOGY)

What, then, is the significance of an eschatological orientation for the way the missionary mandate is performed? The first consequence to be drawn by the missionary community and single agent is one of *joyful assurance*. The outcome of the work in which we are engaged is not open-ended and endangered. Christ, the risen Lord, assures his messengers he will at no time leave them alone but will be with them until the end of this age (Matt 28:20). This means that the work of world evangelization is based on the truth that Christ's *historical victory* at the cross and in his resurrection will be crowned by his *final victory*, when he returns in glory and finally will destroy every antagonistic rule and every authority and power (1 Cor 15:28).

Second, eschatological orientation inspires missionaries with a sense of *urgency*. Since the final victory of Christ and the establishment of his Kingdom in glory is a salvational event utterly to be longed for, and since its coming to pass is conditioned by the execution of the universal missionary mandate, no other duty is of comparable importance to that of reaching those who have not heard the gospel but must hear it before Christ can come back. This sense of urgency is the distinguishing mark of the genuine missionary spirit ever since the apostle to the nations, Paul, made it his ambition to preach the gospel where nobody had preached it before and never settled at any place where he had already preached and established a Christian bridgehead (Rom 15:20).

Third, eschatological orientation makes the gospel a *message of hope* also to those who come to hear it. Heathen are those persons who are "without God and without hope in the world" (Eph 2:12), although they might give themselves to various illusions that are bound to end in disappointment and despair. Often they are lacking also a sense of history, and therefore find it difficult to lead a purposeful life. Thus, it can be proved historically that with the arrival of the Christian gospel whole cultures have become dynamized and tribes and nations have become involved in constructing a new society and building up an independent nation.

Fourth, since eschatological hope is a hope which is anticipated partly already by the renewing force of God's eschatological installment—*the gift of the Holy Spirit*—missions are able and called to erect *signs of the Kingdom*. Such signs are, first of all, renewed human lives that exhibit something of the glorious liberty of the children of God. The most important corporate sign is the *indigenous church* and an *eschatological community* which in the mutual love of her members across all former social and cultural barriers anticipates the great crowd out of all tribes and nations that will be assembled before the throne of the Lamb. Missions, therefore, does not end with the sowing of the good seed and the conversion of individuals, but will take great care to plant vigorous churches that truly exhibit the victorious life granted within Christ's Kingdom of grace here on earth. Members of such a church will be actively involved as responsible citizens in their national society and will work towards ethical transformation which restores the dignity of men and women who are created to be God's images.

Fifth, at the same time that eschatological orientation releases impulses to shoulder socio-ethical responsibility, it also cautions the evangelist to exhibit a *sense of patience*. The proper object of eschatological hope is God's Kingdom in glory. That Kingdom will be established only at the return of Christ, who will implement it by completing the spiritual redemption of our sinful bodies (Rom 8:23) as well as by annihilating or exiling the still existing forces of sin, Devil and death (1 Cor 15:24). This acts as a *warning against making empty inner-worldly promises and pursuing utopian social projects* which might collapse into failure and consequently turn the national spirit against the seemingly fraudulent Christian faith. Above all, this eschatological caution prevents us from changing the gospel into a humanistic ideology.

Sixth, eschatological orientation makes the missionary community watchful to *discern the spirit of Antichrist*. In his pursuit to set up his own final reign, that person is already now working in the world. Trust in the eschatological coming of our saving King makes us courageous in facing the counterattacks of the satanic enemy who does not freely surrender his strongholds (especially pagan cults) to the saving rule of Christ. I believe it is extremely important for missiologists to develop a *theology of religions* and a strategy to meet them which is *aware of the demonic component* of all non-Christian religions and ideologies and their anti-Christian invigoration in connection with the approach of the final clash.[18]

Finally, the most important consequence of an eschatological orientation for the missionary task force is to realize *the primacy of prayer and ardent intercession* as a prerequisite to the missionary encounter.[19] By prayer we plead the promises of God given to his obedient people, and we anticipate the coming of our Lord in power and glory. Prayer confident in the *parousia* releases some of the divine spiritual dynamite which one day will come to subject all creation to the rule of the Lord and make all things new (Rev 21:5).

CHAPTER TWO

WORLD EVANGELIZATION AND THE KINGDOM OF GOD

INTRODUCTION

What vision inspires us when we meet to consider the evangelization of the world in our generation? Surely it is that this troubled world will finally see the Kingdom of God.

But what exactly do we mean when we speak of the Kingdom of God as the goal of evangelism? Do we think mainly of a spiritual event which takes place hidden in the hearts of men, or do we refer to a new order of the world? Would such a new world order become realized here and now, or do we see it as a future event for which we can only hope? In what way can our evangelistic action contribute to the establishment of God's Kingdom?

The purpose of this chapter is, first, in a number of propositions, to redefine on biblical grounds the nature of evangelism in relation to the Kingdom of God; second, to clarify this biblical concept over against its present-day distortions; and, third, to indicate the practical consequences which follow our evangelistic action in the present situation.

PART I: EVANGELIZATION—INVITING INTO THE KINGDOM OF GRACE

1. The gospel which Jesus preached to the Jews was "glad tidings" to them as it announced the fulfillment of Israel's central hope, the final establishment of God's messianic rule.

The proclamation of the Kingdom of God (the Kingdom of Heaven) forms the heart of the evangelistic ministry of Jesus (Matt 4:17) and his apostles. Jesus points to the Kingdom as the very reason for his coming: "I must evangelize about the Kingdom of God in the other cities also; for I was sent for this purpose" (Luke 4:43).

Why did Jesus choose this idea of God's Kingdom as his favorite theme? The German scholar Wilhelm Bousset has rightly stated, "The sum total of everything which Israel expected of the future was the Kingdom of God."[1] Jesus, therefore, did not introduce a new idea when speaking about the Kingdom. Rather, he referred to the most important concept of Israel's belief and hope. The OT had left the Jews with one basic problem: on the one hand, Israel had always believed and confessed that her God is already the sovereign Ruler over his whole creation. More especially he had chosen Israel to participate in his rule by their becoming a kingdom of priests among all nations (Exod 19:5-6). On the other hand, Israel also experienced that the nations did not recognize God's rule. At times God did not even seem to be able to protect his own people from the attacks of its heathen enemies. Was God a King without a Kingdom?

The answer which was given to Israel through the prophets was this: it was on account of Israel's own disobedience against God's holy commandments that the special covenant was broken. Therefore, God has delivered the Israelites into the hands of the Gentile nations. But God does not give up his intention to make the whole earth the place of his glory and to use Israel to establish his rulership over all nations. The day will come when God again will demonstrate his power and manifest himself as the supreme King of the earth. He will intervene in the course of history and change the lot of his people. This will be on the so-called Day of the Lord. The Day of the Lord stands for the great series of eschatological

events when God finally will restore his people Israel both spiritually and physically. God will pour out his Spirit on his people to
bring about a spiritual regeneration (Ezek 37:9-10; 39:29; Joel
2:28-29; Zech 12:10). He will send the Messiah to be the agent of
salvation. Through him God will establish his reign of peace on
Mount Zion. This rule will extend to all nations on earth (Isa 2:1-
5; 9:1-7; 11:1-16). Voluntarily the kings will come to Jerusalem to
worship the God of Israel and to accept his laws. And thus they will
live in peace, justice and prosperity. This is what the words "Malkut
JAHWEH"—i.e., the Kingdom of the Lord—meant to the
Israelites.

And now we make two important observations:

The first observation is that it is exactly in connection with the
prophetic announcement of the "Day of the Lord" that the concept
of evangelism is born in OT times. The word "evangelize" is used
for the first time in its typically biblical meaning in the 52nd and
61st chapters of Isaiah. The prophet receives a vision which he is
urged to proclaim to his people. He sees the Lord return to Zion
and take up his universal reign (52:7-8). The office of the evangelist himself assumes a messianic character. He becomes spiritually
identified with the expected Messiah, whose ministry again is
described as a prophetic function. A marvelous message of eschatological salvation forms the content of this evangelism: "The Spirit
of the Lord is upon me, because the Lord has anointed me to evangelize (i.e., to bring good tidings to) the afflicted; he has sent me to
bind up the brokenhearted, to proclaim liberty to the captives . . .
to proclaim the year of the Lord's favour, the day of vengeance of
our God; to comfort all who mourn" (61:1-2).

Our second observation is this: the same prophetic understanding of evangelism as announcing the Kingdom of God breaking liberatingly into history is taken up in the NT Gospels again.
But there are some decisively new elements in the NT understanding of the Kingdom. Jesus himself called these new elements the
mysteries (or secrets) of the Kingdom (Matt 13:11) which he
unfolded in his own teaching.

2. The Kingdom which is proclaimed in NT evangelism is centered in Jesus Christ.

In his sermon in the synagogue of Nazareth (Luke 4:16-20) Jesus identifies himself with the messianic prophet of Isa 61:1—"The Spirit of the Lord God is upon me, because the Lord anointed me to evangelize the afflicted." His startling comment on this famous text is, "Today the scripture has been fulfilled in your hearing!"

This does not mean that the Kingdom as it was expected so anxiously by the Jews had been totally established by the work of Jesus (realized eschatology). There is not that drastic change in history and nature yet which will mark the *shalom*, the peace, of the messianic Kingdom. But his proclamation and his works demonstrate vital elements of it. They are not the Kingdom in full, but they are signs which point to Jesus himself as the bringer of this Kingdom. In fact, he is the most important and central element of the Kingdom. All the gifts of the messianic Kingdom are contained in the person of Jesus Christ and mediated through his messianic ministry. It is a ministry rather different from the spectacular political expectations of the contemporary Jews (especially of the Pharisees and the Zealots), for it culminates in the vicarious death of the Messiah (Matt 16:21-27). This appears scandalous even to his own disciples, although it was predicted in the Servant Songs of Isaiah (especially chapter 53). But this is the peculiar way in which the Kingdom of God was to be ushered in according to the plan of God.

Therefore, all evangelism which is carried out by the apostles and the Early Church is Christ-centered. In fact, it has rightly been observed[2] that in the writings of Paul and John the very place which Jesus in his evangelism gave to the Kingdom is now filled by Jesus himself (2 Cor 1:20). It is Christ's coming, his atoning death, his victorious resurrection, and his glorious return which now form the main pillar of evangelistic preaching both to the Jews and Gentiles. "For Jews demand signs and Greeks wisdom, but we preach Christ crucified" (1 Cor 1:22).

Christ must, therefore, remain the center of *our* evangelism as well. And it must be the authentic Christ as he is proclaimed and taught in the apostolic writings of the NT. The great danger in many churches' mission today is that they reverse God's way from the Old to the NT. The OT descriptions of the gifts of the Kingdom, liberation, and eschatological *shalom* have been rediscovered. But often they are isolated from Christ as the bringer and the Lord of the Kingdom and from the way in which he accomplished the restoration of God's rule over men. This is the nature of a post-Christian ideology. It is shocking to discover how today some theologians and church leaders even draw parallels between NT salvation and that salvation which is brought or promised by present-day ideologies and religions. Jesus, as far as he is still referred to by them, is reduced to the type of liberator who from Cyrus to Mao Tse-tung has many important parallels. This is a terrible distortion of the biblical gospel of the Kingdom. For even if the Kingdom as promised by the prophets were already realized visibly, it would be of no avail to us if Jesus were not to be found in it (Psa 73:25).

3. *Christian evangelism preaches a Kingdom that is realized now by spiritual regeneration.*

Another distinct mark in the NT understanding of the Kingdom is that in its deepest nature it is spiritual. This does not renounce the expectation that one day it will also come with visible force, "with power and great glory" (Matt 24:30), and that it will reshape the whole physical world as well. But its basic structure is not physical (Rom 14:17). We may define the NT understanding of the Kingdom as follows: the Kingdom of God is God's redeeming Lordship successively winning such liberating power over the hearts of men that their lives and thereby finally the whole creation (Rom 8:21) become transformed into childlike harmony with his divine will.

This is the reason the Kingdom of God could never be established by political action. And since sinful man by nature is opposed to the will of God, it cannot even be brought about by moral education. The acknowledgment of God's rule presupposes a miraculous change of heart which can be achieved only by an intervention of God himself.

At the cross of Jesus Christ God has made peace between the sinful world and himself. Through the gifts of the Holy Spirit poured out on the day of Pentecost and henceforth bestowed on each repentant believer (Acts 2:38; 1 Cor 12:7, 11), God makes it possible for men to accept his offer of reconciliation and to live a victorious new life in childlike communion with him (Rom 8:1-27).

The invitation to receive this wonderful offer is the basic function of Christian evangelism. The evangelist, commissioned by Christ himself, offers God's grace to a mankind whose essential misery is its righteous condemnation by God (2 Cor 5:17-21). And those who, aided by the Holy Spirit, accept the message of reconciliation are already entering the Kingdom of God (Matt 10:15; 21:31). Having become members of the invisible Kingdom of grace now, they will, if they endure, most surely be partakers in the messianic rule when the Kingdom comes in power and glory.

This spiritual nature of the Kingdom has always been stressed by evangelicals, even in view of the demands for its social realization. The suffering under the injustice and oppression in the present state of world affairs and the cry for liberation and peace are needs which burn in the hearts of conscientious people at all times and in all cultures. In response to this, new religions and ideologies have emerged, and social and political movements for drastic changes in society have been founded. Today the quest for total renewal is resounding with even greater vigor than before. Some churches are responding to it through so-called church renewal movements. But the crucial question is, "Renewal how?" Is it through a return to the Word of God or through group dynamics and ideological indoctrination?

More and more influential Christians today are inclined to side with the Marxists, who believe that the reason for all oppression and violence is to be found in the economic laws inherent in our present capitalistic system and the wrong distribution of power in the established world society, especially in Europe and North America. Revolutionary change of all social and political structures would then be the answer. In Bangkok 1973 even the churches were called upon to become "renewed" by ridding themselves of the "captivity of power in the North Atlantic Community."

Evangelicals will agree that the concentration of executive power and finances can corrupt. Far too often they have not been aware of the social and political side of moral evil and its institutional perpetuation. But the basic fallacy of Marxism and any other kind of humanistic ideology of salvation is that it believes in the inherent goodness of human nature. Therefore, the results accomplished by such types of revolutionary renewal are very often the appearance of the same selfish and heartless oppression now shifted into the hands of the revolutionaries of yesterday.

The renewal which God has to offer is a far more radical one. It is the renewal of our mind by being regenerated and transformed to the mind of Jesus Christ (Rom 12:2). This offer by far exceeds all other human solutions. This offer is made in evangelism. The total ministry of Jesus consisted in teaching, evangelizing and healing (Matt 5:23; 9:35; 10:7-8). Evangelism has one specific function in this total missionary ministry: it is decisively to ignite the desire for new life in Christ. But as soon as this life is born, it will express itself in the works of love (Gal 5:6). We should never allow ourselves to distrust the worth of God's offer through our evangelistic ministry and secretly exchange our birthright for an ideological pottage of lentils.

Neither should it be argued that such spiritual renewal remains merely internal or individualistic. Perhaps sometimes evangelicals have been tempted to reduce the gifts of renewal to this dimension. But this is a caricature of true evangelical understanding of the gifts of the Kingdom. If a man is really renewed in Christ, this renewal will start internally with him. This is and remains true. But if this new spiritual life develops in a healthy way, it will make itself felt in all spheres of a man's life and social involvements. The interhuman relations of Christians are the links between personal regeneration and the transformation of society through the forces of the Kingdom (Matt 5:13-16). Truly regenerated Christians are better citizens, for their Christian life also generates in them a new spontaneousness and creativity in moral action, a new responsibility in public positions entrusted to them, and the desire to bring about reconciliation, solidarity and mutual participation. This has already been proved many times in history. I am thinking of the evangelical contributions to the abolition of slavery and the social reforms for the protection of widows and orphans, or the institution of the diaconate of charity.

What *practical conclusions* should we draw from this insight? There are two:

First, *the offer of regenerating spiritual power is to be authenticated by the messenger's own spiritual life.* The whole Christian community needs a new awakening and strengthening of its life by the Holy Spirit. Only then can we be joyful witnesses of the good news of salvation. The Holy Spirit came into our hearts when we were born again; but often we block his working by disobeying God and by neglecting to foster our spiritual lives. Such an inner blockage is broken when the Word of God preached to us drives us to repentance and new dedication. Let us, therefore, conduct "missions to missions." Small cells and regular gatherings such as the Keswick Convention should be encouraged which concentrate on the task of reviving the worker's inner life by Bible messages, counseling and prayer.

Second, *evangelical missions ought to develop convincing models of social and political involvement which are generated and directed by Christ's redeeming love.* Personal contact with the people with whom we share the new life will unveil both their spiritual and their bodily needs. If we approach the latter ones, we should show that physical, social, economic and political problems too are rooted in fallen man's thirst for God as the fountain of life. On the other hand, true evangelism will show that no single aspect of human life and suffering lies outside the concern of Christ and his Church. Here the doctrine of the different gifts and assignments of the members of Christ's body should be developed practically. This leads us to our next biblical proposition.

4. *Evangelism leads into the Church as the new messianic community of the Kingdom.*

One of the intricate questions of NT theology is the relation between the Kingdom of God and the Church. There are two extremes in answering this question. The high-church tradition on the one side has tended to equate the Kingdom with the Church. Everything a mission does should contribute to establishing and developing the Church. On the other side, there are those liberal theologians who, with Bultmann, maintain that Jesus was so obsessed by the belief in the imminent coming of the Kingdom that he never intended to establish a Church.[3]

The truth is that the messianic Kingdom presupposes a messianic community—the specific people of God, destined to exercise the messianic ministry to the rest of the nations.

The Church is not identical with the Kingdom of God. But she is the transitory communal form of it in the present age, and through his Church Christ exercises a most important ministry towards the visible coming of the Kingdom. She is the new Israel, the messianic community of the New Covenant: "You are a chosen race, a royal priesthood, a holy nation, God's own people, that you may declare the wonderful deeds of him who called you out of darkness into his marvellous light" (1 Pet 2:9).

This is of tremendous importance for our understanding of *evangelism*. The goal of evangelism is not only to make individual believers, but to persuade believers to live as responsible members in the Church, God's messianic community. In the total task of mission, the work of evangelism is continued by the planting of local churches in each nation. Even as a small minority, such a church is to be regarded as the first fruit of Christ's saving love for the whole people and will, therefore, be established on a self-multiplying basis (church growth).

This brings us to the task of *church education*. The task of mission is not only to gather new converts into the churches, but to help these churches grow into their full maturity. This means developing the internal life of the church by deepening believers' spiritual knowledge and fellowship and relating the church to the needs of the environment. Bible classes, Bible schools, Christian academies, and leadership training centers will have to fulfill a decisive role in educating Christians to become responsible members of their churches rather than sheep who simply are attended to.

New insistence on the role of the priesthood of all believers must not divert our concern for improving theological education for the ministry of the younger churches. Modern Protestant missions have been working towards the complete nationalization of the ordinary ministry of the churches which they have planted. This means they must have fully indigenous leadership at all levels (shepherds and teachers) who are able to uphold, defend and spread the Christian faith both in genuine continuity with the historic tradition and in relevant relation to the specific environment of these churches.

PART II: EVANGELIZATION—PREPARING THE KINGDOM OF GLORY

Genuine Christian faith in the Kingdom has always been marked by an awareness that is joyful and painful at the same time. It is joy because the Kingdom of grace has come with the first arrival of Christ. And it is pain in that Christ has not yet come again to establish his Kingdom in power and glory by demonstrating his victory before the eyes of all mankind. There is still something which contradicts the Lordship of Jesus Christ.

1. *The opposition between the Kingdom of God and the kingdom of Satan necessarily involves the evangelist in warfare.*

When we see the role of evangelism within the framework of God's coming Kingdom, we must still consider the existence of that opposing metaphysical army which the Gospel of John says is led by "the prince of this world" (John 12:31; 14:30; 16:11). The world which is to be won for the Kingdom of Christ through evangelism is not a neutral territory. It is rather in a state of active rebellion. The idolatrous religions of men are ways Satan seduces the heathen to worship him (1 Cor 10:20; 2 Cor 6:16). Their personal, cultural and social life is under demonic captivity, where love of God and one's neighbor is replaced by suspicion and hostility (Rom 1:24-30). This grim fact gives a dramatic notion to the concepts both of the

Kingdom of Christ and of evangelism. The advancement of the Kingdom of Christ takes place by a successive dethronement of Satan (Luke 10:17-19). The decisive victory has already been won on the cross, where Satan lost his legal rights over mankind (John 12:31). Evangelism, therefore, is accompanied by battle with satanic forces (Matt 10:1, 8). It is to proclaim over them the victory of Christ and to command them to depart.

But according to the testimony of the NT, the power of Satan on earth has not been annihilated yet, nor will it be before the glorious return of Christ. Nor will the totality of mankind be won over from Satan's dominion to the Kingdom of Christ. Evangelism calls for a decision. The Holy Spirit gives us the freedom to say "yes," but he also leaves to us the liberty to say "no." Therefore, the final result of evangelism is not the unification of mankind under the rule of Christ but, on the contrary, a growing polarization between the Kingdom of God and the kingdom of Satan.

One of the most fatal errors in mission work is the idea that it is our task in this present age (before the visible reappearance of Christ) to Christianize the world and thereby to establish the messianic Kingdom by our own power. Such mistaken Christians are directed by the utopian vision of a unified mankind in which perfect peace and justice have become a universal reality now. They are, however, frustrated by the fact that a great part of mankind simply refuses to accept the gospel and to live according to the new Law of Christ's Kingdom. Therefore, they despair of the efficiency of purely spiritual means—i.e., an evangelistic method which relies wholly on the challenging impression of the Word of God on the human conscience.

Two dangerous alternatives are offered to an eschatologically-oriented evangelism. The first one is the development of *a misdirected form of evangelism* which in order to achieve striking visible results resorts to *psychological methods* such as mass hypnosis, group dynamics experiments, personality cults, or even tapping into parapsychological forces disguised as the work of the Holy Spirit. Some people try to attract their listeners by material benefits or by the promise of spectacular healing or earthly prosperity which will follow their conversion. There is no real blessing in such work. It might even drive the evangelist himself into secret cynicism and loss of his faith.

The other equally mistaken alternative is offered by Christians who replace the messianic Kingdom with *a utopian vision* to be realized by *political means*. They repeat the error of the Zealots at the time of Jesus, who wanted to force the Kingdom of God to come by ejecting the Romans by the sword. The physical resources of the Christian churches do not, of course, suffice to remove all forces of oppression. Therefore, some even advocate an alliance with the liberation movements within non-Christian religions and ideologies. This new concept of "mission" is today's greatest menace to the worldwide Church. I would call it the "Mission of Barabbas." It has no promise from the Lord. It might, however, achieve at least a transitory success. But such a worldwide kingdom which is achieved by the combined spirits, concepts, and methods of the dynamic movements of this age would be a kingdom without Christ. It would be the anti-Christian kingdom.

And this is what we, in fact, have to expect. The NT clearly predicts that in spite of great victories of the gospel amongst all nations, the resistance of Satan will continue. Towards the end it will even increase so much that Satan, controlling the human person of Antichrist, will assume once more an almost total control over disobedient mankind (2 Thess 2:3-12; Revelation 13). It is important to notice the religious appearance of the reign of Antichrist. He will gain his hold over mankind not only by military or political force but also through the magic enchantments of his false prophet (Rev 13:11-17). But God has given us a weapon with which to resist. It is the sword of the Spirit (Eph 6:17), the Word of God. It is the testimony of the martyrs that through Christ's victory on the cross Satan has lost his dominion (Rev 12:11-12).

I am afraid that many evangelical Christians are not yet prepared or equipped to fight this battle. We need new biblical clarity in order to be reassured of our evangelistic motivation and to be able to discern the spirits. Today Satan attacks churches, missions, and individual Christians all over the world by heretical movements which threaten them with spiritual confusion. The Declarations of Wheaton[4] and Frankfurt[5] have undertaken to penetrate this smoke screen theologically. The issues mentioned in these historic statements ought to be taken up at all levels of the worldwide mission. They must be answered by way of affirmation and refutation in clear-cut confessional statements which are binding on our evangelistic activities and identify us in the eyes of our Christian supporters.

2. Evangelism is inspired by the vision of the Kingdom in glory which will be established through the return of Christ.

Evangelism comes to men with a present offer based upon Christ's victory on the cross, and with an eschatological promise based on his final victory at his return. This dialectical tension within the historical movement of God's Kingdom is the driving dynamic of evangelism. It offers God's grace in Christ and new life in the Holy Spirit now. It promises total redemption of our bodies and of the whole creation in the Kingdom of glory to come. Paul says that the whole "creation waits with eager longing for the revealing of the sons of God . . . because the creation itself will be set free from its bondage and obtain the glorious liberty of the children of God" (Rom 8:19-20). This will take place at the return of Christ. He will transform his militant Church into his triumphant Church which will reign together with him in his messianic Kingdom of universal peace (Matt 19:28-29; Luke 22:28-30; 1 Cor 6:2; Rev 20:4). This eschatological notion has always been the distinct mark of a truly biblical understanding of evangelism. It has inspired many missionaries with a holy restlessness.

But there is one question which is controversial even amongst evangelicals. We have already touched on this in our first chapter, pleading not to exaggerate the divisiveness of this issue, but rather to understand the specific valid concerns in each of the well-known basic positions. Still, the theological problem must be faced: What will be the exact nature of the Kingdom which Christ will establish at his return? Will it be the totally new heaven and new earth which John describes in Revelation 21 and 22 (Amillennialism)? Or will it be the millennium which he mysteriously speaks about in Rev

20:1-6 (Premillennialism)? The biblical texts give us material support but also difficulty for both of these views.

Amillenarians understand Rev 20:1-6 not literally but symbolically. They hold that we live in the millennium now, or rather at the end of it, when Satan is loosed again. The risen saints would be those who after their victorious death are united with Christ now in heaven, although their bodies are not yet resurrected.

Premillenarians conceive the Kingdom in power which the returning Christ will establish as an anticipation of the final Kingdom in glory. It will only come when even death has been swallowed up into victory (1 Cor 15:24-26).

Still another attempt to solve the apparent tension between the different eschatological texts (e.g., Rev 20:1-6 and 2 Pet 3:10) is Postmillennialism. Here the millennium is the last victorious phase of church history before the return of Christ. It brings an almost universal recognition of the gospel amongst the nations through a new outpouring of the Holy Spirit. But it is difficult to reconcile such a view with the clear biblical prediction of the numerical shrinkage and tribulation of the church at the close of this age. Jesus himself prophesies that the very survival of the elect will be threatened (Matt 24:21-31). The persecutor is Antichrist, whom "the Lord Jesus will slay with the breath of his mouth and destroy by his appearing and his coming" (2 Thess 2:8). In fact, are not these apocalyptical features becoming visible even before our own eyes? Is not the shadow of Antichrist falling on us already? Where do postmillenarians place his appearance? Unless they provide us with an answer to this question, their view of the millennium can hardly be called biblical.

Personally I am inclined to agree with a modified premillenarian view which meets the confessional criticism directed against Chiliasm as a materialistic form of the millennium. The parousia— i.e., the appearance of Christ—is not a plain melding of the invisible and the visible realms of Christ's reign into a political theocracy where he and his saints permanently reside on our old earth again. Rather, we should understand the parousia as the climactic encounter of the yet invisible Lordship of Christ with present world history. Thereby the dividing wall between here and beyond, between now and then, will become transparent for a definite period, until all cosmic power has been subdued to Christ (1 Cor 15:25-26) and world history is swallowed up by the new creation.

Only God's final fulfillment of the biblical prophecies will bring us the solution to all exegetical problems. In any case, the controversy between amillenarians and premillenarians need not affect our understanding of evangelism as urgently oriented toward the appearance of Christ's coming with his Kingdom in power and glory. General agreement already exists on two key points: First, that Christ will establish this Kingdom only after he has evangelized the nations through our instrumentality (Matt 24:14; Mark 13:10; Acts 1:6-8); second, that churches and missions have to be watchful against the anti-Christian temptation (Matt 24:4, 11, 23-36).

3. *The crowning link between the evangelization of the world and the establishment of the messianic Kingdom will be the restoration of Israel.*

Why do I believe that the millennium is an intervening period between the return of Christ and the creation of a new heaven and a new earth? It is because of the specific role which the OT has assigned to the people of Israel within the messianic Kingdom. These prophecies have not yet been fulfilled, nor have they been nullified by the creation of the Church as the new spiritual Israel (Acts 1:6). Paul in Rom 11:29 very definitely states that the gifts and the call of God to Israel are irrevocable. He clearly predicts the final conversion of the historic Israel. This reinclusion in the olive tree of the earthly people of God will mean great riches for the Gentile nations (v. 12).

Now there is an important threefold relationship between the Church's world evangelism to the Gentile nations and the final acceptance of the people of Israel. First, Paul states that one vital purpose in his ministry to the Gentiles is to make his fellow Jews jealous of his salvation in Christ (Rom 11:11-14). This means that our evangelistic work should always be done with an eye cast desirously on the promised salvation of the Jews as well. This

Christian witness to Israel must always accompany mission to the Gentiles.

The second connection is the mystery that the present hardening of Israel will cease when the full number of the Gentiles has come in (v. 25). This actually means that the *time of world evangelism is limited*. The times of grace for the Gentiles are exactly the interval between the hardening of Israel which followed their rejection of their Messiah and his gospel, and their eschatological restoration which will, according to Ezek 37:8-10, first be physical and thereafter spiritual.

The third connection between the Church's mission to the Gentiles and the restoration of Israel is of vital importance to our understanding of the *limitation of our task* in world evangelism. Israel's conversion will mark the transformation from world evangelization to world christianization. The Church's assignment in the present dispensation is not to take the world of nations politically under the Law of Christ as expressed in the Sermon on the Mount. Under the present conditions, with Satan still unbound, this simply is not possible. But in the messianic reign Satan will be bound and not able to deceive the nations any more (Rev 20:3). Therefore, the rule of peace exercised through the ministry of Israel from Mount Zion will also establish a long-lasting political peace. Meanwhile, however, world evangelism has only one direct purpose: to gather the eschatological community of the elect out of all nations.

That Israel forms the decisive eschatological linkage between world evangelism and the establishment of the messianic Kingdom is a prophetic insight especially exciting to our present generation. Jesus has said to the Jews: "Jerusalem will be trodden down by the Gentiles, until the (appointed) time (of grace—*kairoi*) of the Gentiles will be fulfilled" (Luke 21:24). This is exciting, for in the year 1967 our very generation became witness to the manner in which Jerusalem in an amazing war was recaptured by the Jews. For the first time since its destruction in A.D. 70 the capital of Israel is not trodden down by the Gentiles. But the Yom Kippur war in 1973 brought about a new turn. Because of the oil boycott of the Arab states nearly all people of the earth started to turn against

Israel, as predicted by the OT prophets (Ezekiel 38; Zech 12:3). Today in its attempt to crush the *Intifada*, Israel finds itself rather isolated internationally. Does this mean that the times of grace for the heathen—i.e., the appointed times for world evangelization— are drawing to their end as well? I believe so. In fact, we are observing this already in many parts of the world.

4. *Reinforced evangelism is the erected sign of victory in the final battle of the Kingdom of Christ with the powers of Antichrist.*

In his apocalyptic sermon on the Mount of Olives about the fate of Jerusalem and the end of world history, Jesus answers what has become a burning question for our generation (Matt 24:3): "When will this be, and what will be the sign of your coming and the close of the age?" Jesus mentions a number of striking signs. They appear in nature and in world history, as well as in the life of the Christian Church: wars, famines, earthquakes, false prophets. They all signal that the end is approaching, but they are not yet the end. Then Jesus comes to the dramatic last phase: the great apostasy in which the love of most men will grow cold (Matt 24:10-12) precedes the great tribulation (vv. 21-22). The final phase of church history will not be marked by great revival movements or by the complete christianization of the nations. On the contrary, only an elect minority will endure and be saved (Matt 24:22, 25). Yet one basic function of the Church will go on even under these circumstances. Nobody will stop it until it has reached its target: "And this gospel of the Kingdom will be preached throughout the whole earth, as a testimony to all nations, and then the end will come" (Matt 24:14). This prophecy puts Christ's commission to evangelize the world into an apocalyptic context. Evangelism is the chief contribution of the Church to hasten the visible establishment of Christ's Kingdom on earth. Only when this work is complete will Christ come to redeem the groaning creation from its present bondage.[6]

The purpose of such eschatological evangelism is not just to make as many converts as possible. In that case statistics would decide the meaning of world evangelization. Our task is not to boast in numerical results (although we may rejoice in them!), for the full number of those who will be saved is known to God alone (John 10:16; Rom 11:25). It must be assumed that the majority of the listeners will not receive our offer of grace. Still, Jesus insists that the gospel of the Kingdom will and must be preached throughout the world until the end. Then people will either be accepted or judged according to their obedience or disobedience to the Word. But eventually every knee in heaven and on earth and under the earth will bow, and every tongue will confess that Christ is the Lord, to the glory of God (Phil 2:10).

What does this mean for our task here and now? Let me conclude by issuing a threefold challenge. First, the still-open doors for the gospel call for an *all-out effort to evangelize all six continents*. Churches and missions should make it their target to reach every living person with the good news. It is clear that we should make the best use of all modern means of communication and prepare excellent programs for radio and TV. But wherever it is legally possible, our evangelistic outreach should culminate in personal visitation and a face-to-face encounter. This means that all believers in a given locality ought to be involved—evangelism in depth!

Second, all such efforts would benefit greatly if they could draw from the experiences of fellow Christians in other parts of the world and if they could be coordinated in a *worldwide strategy*. This should include all churches, mission societies, Christian groups, and individuals who sincerely believe that the proclamation of the undiluted gospel to the unreached two billion is our most important task in this decisive hour of world history. Therefore, I wholeheartedly support the proposals made by many to make it one strategical goal to reach all hitherto unreached peoples by A.D. 2000—if this is not continued with an apocalyptic prophecy!—and to coordinate the various schemes as much as possible.

Third, we do not know, however, how much time we still have to prepare such bold plans for world evangelization. God's mission can express itself in our plans, but he is not bound by them. On the contrary, his mission can proceed even in a situation of persecution where organized missions are no longer possible. There he uses, instead, the confessing testimony of individual Christians and small groups. Until recently this was the situation in countries behind the Iron Curtain. Let us support by our intercessions all our persecuted brethren and sisters wherever they may be. And let us prepare ourselves and our constituencies for such times, as martyrdom may be expected of *us* too. For it is "through many tribulations we must enter the Kingdom of God" (Acts 14:22).

CHAPTER THREE

GOD'S KINGDOM AND MODERN UTOPIANISM
A Biblical Encounter with Some Contemporary Philosophical and Theological Systems

The historical dimension of the future has entered the mind of modern man with new urgency. It constitutes both a fascinating and a frightening force. On the one hand, during the sixties we witnessed a strong wave of futurist optimism. This was expressed in a number of philosophical and theological systems, but also in sociopolitical movements and ecclesiastical events. Early in the seventies, however, the pendulum was swinging back. Suddenly one became frighteningly aware that the same forces and attempts that promised to make the future "the land of unlimited possibilities" might just as easily throw our earth into an ecological disaster. The new question is: how are we to avert this menace?

Both reactions—the enthusiastic hope of the utopia of world change and the worried prognoses associated with cybernetics—have been taken up by the churches as a challenge. For the future is a central perspective in the biblical message. The worries about the safety and well-being of threatened mankind, on the other hand, must also stir up Christian responsibility for decisive action. Thus, we understand why the topic "the future" has become the first priority for the Ecumenical Movement. At the same time, the difference in eschatology constitutes a central aspect of that fundamental gap which separates evangelical from modernist theologians today as two broad currents of world Christianity. Therefore, reexamining our evangelical position over against non-Christian concepts can greatly clarify the spiritual situation.

PART I: THE FUTURE AS FASCINATION AND AS NIGHTMARE

The Goals of Messianic Marxism

Amongst the neo-Marxists there is one school of thought which has been called "messianic Marxism." Its representatives were the first Marxist-Communists who were willing to open up a constructive dialogue with Christian theologians. This Marxist-Christian conversation reached its climax during the sixties. It suffered a great setback when it was condemned by the mouthpieces of established "'orthodox' Marxism"—i.e., by the Communist parties. The hopes set on this dialogue were almost shattered by the invasion of the Red Army of the CSSR in August 1968. Yet the talk is going on, especially through the Paulus Society.[1] At least for the Christian side its significance is still growing, and in Latin America it has given birth to the "Theology of Liberation"[2] as the dominant school of thought.

The importance of the concept of the messianic Marxists for our theme is this: Although they do cling to the premises of philosophic materialism, they have received decisive new impulses from studying the Bible. In the OT prophets and in the preaching of Jesus about the Kingdom, they discovered a peculiar ardent hope for the future which they saw intimately related to the whole revolutionary history and to the basic concerns of Socialism. Ernst Bloch has called this emotional force the "Wärmestrom"[3] (warm current) of Marxism. Its complementary parallel is the "Kältestrom" (cold current), consisting in socioeconomic analyses and prognoses of dialectic materialism. Both currents need each other in order to preserve the psychological dynamics as well as the critical realism in Marxism. For this synthesis between reflection and enthusiasm Bloch coined the term "Realutopie," thereby giving recognized status to the word "utopia" in Marxist ideology. This "warm current" or "warm red" is the indestructible hope of a new and better life, hope for a coming transformation of all things and a golden age on earth. It is the specific concern of "esoteric Marxism" in general and of the Christian-Marxist dialogue in particular to regain those humanistic dynamics.

The most important representatives of messianic Marxism are the late Tübingen professor Ernst Bloch, the two Czechs Vitezslav Gardavsky and Milan Machovec, and the Frenchman Roger Garaudy, former chief ideologist of the French Communist Party (who later became a convert to Islam because of its futuristic orientation!). Ernst Bloch is the profoundest philosophical thinker amongst them. In three volumes he presented the "Principle of Hope"[4] as the decisive drive in human history. Bloch also inspired Jürgen Moltmann to write his "Theology of Hope"[5] and thereby indirectly gained penetrating influence on ecumenical thought. Roger Garaudy,[6] however, became the more important partner of dialogue for the WCC during the seventies. In his writings the new "Christomarxism," which is spreading with contagious vehemence, has found its classical expression. What are the main thoughts of messianic Marxism?

The starting point is dissatisfaction with the present state of the world. Garaudy sees contemporary society engulfed by a total crisis: "Our society is in a process of dissolution. It calls for a radical change not only of property rights and power structures, but also of our culture and education, of religion and faith, of life and its meaning." Our task is defined by the subtitle of Garaudy's main work: "*Changer la monde et la vie.*"[7] This most needed total change can and must take place only on this earth within our human history. "Human history is the only place where God's Kingdom is to be established,"[8] says Garaudy in the first of his three postulates. This implies the rejection of metaphysical transcendence.

The existence of God is rejected too. Bloch categorically states as basic presupposition "that no God remains in the height, since no God is there at all or ever has been."[9] Atheism is stressed emphatically in order to secure man's responsibility for ushering in the new age. Inasmuch as it is a protest against the Christian quietism in social affairs, this atheism is justified also by Moltmann.[10]

Paradoxically enough, the Bible is not rejected within such atheism. On the contrary, it is praised as an unparalleled source document of hope which really carries the force of change. Bloch tries to resolve that contradiction by an incredible maneuver; in his book *Atheism in Christianity* (1968)[11] he develops the thesis that man's emancipation towards the complete denial of God is the secret theme of the Bible itself! The tempting persuasion of the snake, "You shall be like God," is revaluated into the first promise given to man. This promise, Bloch proposes, was fulfilled by Jesus: "He who sees me, sees the Father." At this point the reinterpretation of the biblical message to annex it to a messianic Marxism reveals its blasphemous nature: "Christ is the symbol of emancipated mankind. . . . In him man for the first time invaded the transcendence and set himself in the place of God, a Messiah against God and for man. . . . Man becomes God, and the greatest sin henceforth is not willing to be like God!"[12]

With the help of such demythologizing (or rather re-mythologizing!) hermeneutics, the Bible becomes one of the most important textbooks of revolution to Marxist readers. Any passage related to God's intervention in history to bring about doom and new creation is read as a challenge to man to follow the example of the "angry Jesus" by siding with the poor and overturning the present power systems of oppression. This approach has been taken over and developed by some theologians as a new hermeneutical key under the name "materialistic exegesis."[13]

More and more statements of biblical faith are being filled with a new ideological content. In particular, the resurrection of Christ is reinterpreted by Garaudy. It becomes the symbol of the new, horizontal transcendence which in neo-Marxist thinking has taken the place of the metaphysical, vertical transcendence. There is no Beyond, no divine reality above us. But there is the historical reality of the future, which lies ahead of us as a possibility to be audaciously seized. Garaudy here speaks of the "eschatological postulate of hope." "Man is a task to be realized; society is a task to be realized; this postulate is congruent with the faith in the resurrection of Christ."[14] Faith in the resurrection, accordingly, is a mental attitude which by courageous actions makes possible what appeared to be impossible. In this attitude one has to undertake decisive steps into the revolutionary tomorrow. Thus Garaudy recognizes his own convictions in the slogan of the Parisian student rebellion in March 1968: "*Soyons raisonable: demandons l'impossible!*"

Thus we see that in messianic Marxism the Kingdom of God has become clearly an entity *within history*, to be *realized by man himself*. Nothing can prevent mankind from opening the gate into the "Kingdom of Liberty" by revolutionary action. The future lies open before us, and reality contains unlimited possibilities which man has to grasp in responsible ventures.

The New World Order of Science and Technology

One of the main reasons messianic Marxists proclaim their principle of earthly hope so optimistically is the immense achievements of technology. Indeed, the last century has witnessed a hectic acceleration of scientific breakthroughs. Nothing seems to remain impossible to *homo faber*. "Anything that can be conceived, can be realized," we are assured by the best-seller *Future Shock*.[15]

This untamable optimism of scientism suffers a glacial chill from the unexpected warnings of well-known experts in various fields, from nuclear physics to food economy. Extrapolating from an immense amount of data, they tell us that our irresponsible exploitation of the earth's resources will drive us into our collective self-destruction.

General alarm was caused by the publication of the two first Reports to the Club of Rome: "Limits of Growth" by Dennis Meadows (1972) and "Mankind at the Turning Point" by Mihailo

Mesarovic and Eduard Pestel (1974).[16] The Club of Rome (founded in 1968) is an informal association of noteworthy scientists, economists, politicians, sociologists and also philosophers who share their reflections upon the future of mankind. Based on their research and computer accounts, they also produce prognoses about the likely effects of uncontrolled progress on the various sectors of life. This is followed by proposals of how to steer these processes into a more responsible direction.

The vision of the future produced by these first two reports to the Club of Rome is gloomy. It could be called a "negative utopia." In his remarkable speech to the Nairobi Assembly in 1975, the Australian biologist Charles Birch summarized the results with a shocking illustration: "The world is like a 'Titanic' on collision course. Ahead of us is an iceberg, whose top appears above the water level. . . . Only a change of course can prevent the disaster."[17] Nothing less than the survival of mankind is at stake!

Although the propositions of the two Reports to the Club of Rome were refuted by other futurologists who have a much more optimistic outlook, one important goal was reached. In the years 1972 and 1974 four large world conferences were convened by the United Nations, and they dealt with the themes mentioned: the Environment Conference in Stockholm (1972), the World Food Conference in Rome, the World Population Conference in Bucharest, and the World Resource Conference in New York (1974). Further congresses were to follow. Yet none of these meetings has led to constructive resolutions which could radically remedy this alarming situation. At the first global conference of the World Future Society at Toronto in September 1980, Dr. Aurelio Peccei, founder of the Club of Rome, told the press: "The world is in a much worse condition than it was ten years ago." Looking back at the seventies, he challenged anyone to show any major area of human affairs where things were going better than ten years earlier. Looking ahead he saw increased problems: The world's population will rise to about six and a half billion by the end of the century, straining still further the planet's declining resources. The economy will decline, the risk of nuclear war will increase, and as forests are cut down, oceans polluted, and deserts expanded, the earth's ability to sustain life will be reduced. Commenting on Peccei's statements, the *Toronto Star* noted:[18] "The world begins more and more to resemble a ricocheting bullet careening from disaster to disaster. . . ." True enough, there are proposals to change the course. The Reports to the Club of Rome were not meant merely to frighten, but also to suggest a program of overcoming the dangers by joint efforts. Charles Birch has mentioned such proposals in Nairobi: zero growth of population, zero growth of products for consumption, zero growth of pollution, and—you could add—zero growth in armaments.

There is one snag in these proposals. They appear rather intriguing, it is true. But they are unrealistic. They break down on account of that opposition which Birch describes as the large invisible part of the iceberg: the social, political and economic structures, as well as the spiritual disorientation about the meaning of life. A way to put it even more clearly is to say, they break down on account of individuals' and human communities' unrestrained desires for possessions, enjoyment and power. Under the present conditions the proposals mentioned cannot be implemented. "No industrialist," says Eduard Ostermann,[19] "no Government, no politician, no manager will accept the proposals of Meadow voluntarily and implement them. It would mean destruction. . . . Some of the effects would be: rise of costs, unemployment, recession, inflation, financial collapse, unrest, social revolution. . . ." The members of the Club of Rome are, of course, aware of this problem. Therefore, their plan is made to include two far-reaching major proposals.

One is to abolish the principle of national states and to replace it by a new international frame, usually referred to as a new political world order and a new economic world order. This was proposed in the third report to the Club of Rome, which was written by twenty-one international experts on national economics and edited in late 1976 by the Dutch Nobel prize winner Jan Tinbergen. Under the title "Reshaping the International Order" (the German title says, "We have but one future—Reform of the International

Order"), the authors suggested replacing the free market economy by a global planning and steering system, for which supra-natural bodies and boards should be created and invested with greater power of decision. "What is required is a new international order in which all benefit from change." De facto this means a step towards a world government.

The other basic proposal is to change man's mentality. Individualism and nationalism must be replaced by a global awareness, through which each person conceives his role as that of a world citizen. In fact, such change of mentality is already attempted by the psychotechnical methods of group dynamics, which are employed in various sections of human life and in industrial management courses, and even in pastoral clinical education and in weekend retreats for congregations.

Now the two utopian proposals have been complemented by a third one, which to us appears even more sensational. The Hungarian-American systems philosopher Erwin Laszlo in 1977 presented the fifth report to the Club of Rome—"Goals for Mankind." Interacting with behaviorists, sociologists, philosophers, theologians and computer specialists, he had been working on a design for a *new world religion*, which should be composed of the helpful elements of all existing religions and ideologies.[20] The volume does not contain the results yet, but it warmly recommends the findings and suggestions of a group called "the religion science-led scenario." Don Hoke remarks:

> The greatest hope for all the world lies in religionists and scientists uniting to awaken the world to its near-fatal predicament and then leading mankind out of the bewildering maze of international crises into the future Utopia of humanist hope.[21]

At least at this point, an eye which is sensitized by biblical revelation discerns the apocalyptic features of this grand program. The Dutch Christian journalist J. A. E. Vermaat writes:

> One day Antichrist is going to push his utopia of unity against the background of total destruction. The frightful vision of dis-

aster shall compel the religions and ideologies to unite. The ideology of the endtime will predominantly be an ideology of survival.[22]

Many will disagree with this judgment. Are we not offered here a futurological design which commends itself by its responsibility, courage and consistency?

If the survival of mankind is really at stake today, and if all organizations and rules by which men have ordered their lives up to now will only speed up our collective destruction, we need radical solutions, they would argue. On the premises of the Club of Rome, it appears that only a world state, ruled by a world government, fed by a planned world economy and inspired by a united world religion or one-world ideology, will be able to bring about that dramatic change of direction which is demanded.

The question put to us, however, is whether we are prepared to share those premises. In the perspective of the Club of Rome, our planet earth is likened to a spaceship which has lost its radar connection with its controlling center on earth, as another Dutchman, A. Schouten, remarks.[23] The crew of this spaceship—mankind— alone is responsible for the continuation of the flight. It must try to grasp hold of its common future and the fate of our earth. But is this the picture which the Bible paints of God's ruling our world and its future?

This question is placed before us by evangelical theologians with great urgency. For today several other political and religious organizations confront us with the same argument and the same goals, offering us their cooperation and asking for ours to solve the problems of our future. We may refer to the World Conference of Religions for Peace, to the United Nations, and (an even greater challenge to us) to the WCC.

The Utopian Vision of the Ecumenical Movement

The original ecumenical goal was to reunite the separated churches. Today this is regarded by leading ecumenicals as just an intermediate stage, as a functional precondition for a much wider goal: the unification of all mankind. This goal was proposed in Uppsala in 1968 under the names "world community" and "new humanity." The ecumenical movement of Geneva today feels the prophetic calling to be pacemaker of a new world order in which the ancient desire of mankind for peace and justice is realized. Here, too, one sees a reinterpretation of the messianic promises in the OT. Since salvation allegedly has been spiritualized and pushed into the Beyond for many centuries, we are asked to rediscover the fuller concept of *shalom* on earth. This goal is, for all influential leaders of the WCC, the motive which, according to Ernst Lange, keeps the Ecumenical Movement moving.[24] In this connection they repeatedly speak of the "ecumenical utopia," the "utopic vision" or of "prophetical dreams." The content is often described by the biblical names of God's Kingdom or the Heavenly Jerusalem. Thus, the WCC too has become a determinately future-oriented movement which lives by a "principle of hope."

This "utopic vision," as the former chairman of the Central Committee, M. M. Thomas, has called it,[25] is propelled by two wings. We could call the left wing liberation, and its nature is basically Marxist inspired. Karl Marx made the "classless society" the goal of history, Ernst Bloch the "kingdom of liberty." Likewise, the Ecumenical Movement dreams of an emancipated world society from which all structures of exploitation and oppression of class, race, economic systems and sex are removed.

This design was largely inspired by neo-Marxist philosophers and sociologists. Their ideas were mediated by their Christian partners in dialogue, theologians such as J. C. Hoekendijk, R. Shaull, J. Moltmann, H. Cox, José Miguez Bonino, and others.[26] Today there are quite a number of conceptions of how to relate the Christian faith to the Marxist ideology of liberation and to fill biblical key terms with Marxist content. We may refer to some of the most commonly known ones: the theologies of revolution, hope and liberation, Black Theology, and, since Melbourne 1980, the "Theology of the Poor."[27] Everywhere Christ is painted as spearheading human liberation from sociopolitical oppression. The liberty sought is taken to be an anticipation, if not indeed the implementation, of the Kingdom of God on earth. "The message of salvation in Christ . . . takes the unavoidable out of our existing national and international institutions and liberates man to the possibility to achieve that new order in which the Kingdoms of the world really become the Kingdom of God and his Christ," wrote Pauline Webb in an introductory article for the 8th World Missionary Conference in Bangkok 1972/73,[28] referring thereby to Roger Garaudy!

The vision of sociopolitical liberation is not left in the abstract. Since 1970 this type of theology (or ideology) has been embodied in concrete action programs into which the real dynamics of the WCC have been channeled. We may mention particularly the Programme of Combating Racism and the Program for Education, which the Marxist educator Paulo Freire[29] introduced to Geneva's third program unit Education and Renewal.

More recently, the often criticized leaning of the WCC towards revolutionary Marxism has been counterbalanced by a new theme, which we could call the right wing of the ecumenical vision. Its name is "One World." That this is the name given to the WCC's popular periodical is not accidental. In Nairobi the class struggle enthusiasm of Geneva's pacemakers seemed to have passed its apex already and was gently overshadowed by the new theme, "Unity of Mankind." Thus, Secretary-General Philip Potter in his report only referred in passing to the liberation theme. Instead, he used the word "global" no fewer than seventeen times! Potter attempted a comprehensive analysis of our contemporary world problems, thereby preempting the lecture of Charles Birch. His conclusion was: "Only a global strategy can solve the global problems of mankind."[30] If, as we saw, the Club of Rome demands the substitution of national by international institutions and tries to awaken a cosmopolitan consciousness, it is gladly assisted by the WCC.

What then should be the specific contribution of the WCC as a religious organization in creating the new international order? First of all, it is busy spreading this idea amongst its member churches. Moreover, it has become a main concern of the WCC to remove all divisions which still stand between various human communities and which block the establishment of a world fellowship.

Break down the walls that separate us
and unite us in a single body

was the chorus sung and danced to with growing enthusiasm at the Fifth Assembly at Nairobi.

The most important activity serving to bring about this unification of mankind is Geneva's Program of Dialogue with Men of Living Faiths and Ideologies. It is to be noted that this Dialogue Program was stimulated in Nairobi by an emphasis on the current threat to human survival.

The new element added at the 5th Assembly was the "spirituality for combat" which M. M. Thomas called for.[31] This included the variety of traditions in Christian piety—starting with the Byzantine liturgy and ending with Pentecostal glossolalia. But the mystical Eastern religions are also being tapped as "spiritual resources" in order to sustain the Ecumenical Movement in its "wanderings through the wilderness" (Potter) towards the unity of mankind.[32] Here an attempt is made in exactly the same direction as that which the leaders of the Club of Rome perceived as a saving solution in the present world crisis. A synthesis of all useful elements in the various religions and ideologies becomes the spiritual fuel which will enable mankind to move towards the goal of global unity. Thus in the present hour of destiny the WCC is allotted an unsought task of highest relevancy. As a "charismatic fellowship," to use Potter's new description of the WCC, it becomes the crystallizing center of uniting humanity. The new spirituality generates that faith which according to Thomas Müntzer, the enthusiastic prophet of the Peasants' Wars in Germany, is the possibility "to attempt the things that seem to be impossible and to complete them."[33] Potter believes that Christians are "called joyfully to join in God's process of creating a new order" and to operate "in concert with God's purpose of transforming his world into his Kingdom of love, joy and peace."[34]

Once more the Kingdom of God and the results of the historic process of global integration into one humanity are openly equated here. At the ecumenical wedding altar, messianic Marxism and futurological doom prophecy are coupled and given a pan-religious inspiration with the purpose of establishing the new world order.

The ecumenical vision constitutes a challenge to all Christians, whether they are affiliated with the WCC or not. Even "conservative evangelicals" are urged to join the venture, as can be seen by all the appeals made to them since Uppsala 1968.

One cannot help being impressed by the ecumenical vision of a better world to be achieved by our united efforts. Its message of impending doom and passionate hope for the future may even remind us of the OT prophets announcing the coming reign of the Lord. But a closer look reveals that such similarities are misleading.

Some Critical Reflections on the Ecumenical Vision

The description of the object of ecumenical hope is void of any serious attempt to recognize the authority of the biblical witness and to examine its authentic contents. Instead, we are offered general human reflections about the present miseries and the aspirations of modern movements for a better future. Together with scientific analyses and prognoses, these are treated as a second source of revelation.

Where the Bible is used—e.g., at ecumenical conferences—it is hermeneutically manipulated by employing the so-called "contextual method." The sociopolitical situation of the reader determines his peculiar interest and leads him to discover just such aspects of the text as seem to provide a relevant answer to his problems. This is done on the basic assumption of materialistic exegetes that the Bible is a textbook of historical records about ancient socioeconomic and political struggles, where God and Jesus were siding with the poor and oppressed who were fighting to liberate themselves. Texts contrary to this tendency are invalidated with the help of ideological criticism, which takes the place of the former idealistic "higher criticism" in the historic-critical method. Since ecumenical hope is estranged from the Bible, it is clearly not fulfilled by the real promises of the prophets. Their place is taken by the idea of an "open future" into which are inserted whatever utopias may be currently fashionable.

Difference in hermeneutics is not the deepest reason for this approach. The dominating ecumenical way of thought is consistent with the entire modern philosophical trend since Hobbes, Hume and Kant to eliminate divine metaphysical transcendence. The history of the empirical world with its inherent forces is regarded as the only objective reality. In the wake of Hegel's philosophy of history, an eschatological dignity is attributed to progress.

The ecumenical vision and the Marxist utopia share the conviction that the Kingdom of God must be realized within this world. Under the influence of Teilhard de Chardin and process philosophy, faith in a personal God who as a sovereign Creator and Redeemer stands transcendentally outside this world is replaced by a new type of panentheism: God is equated with the creative process in the horizontal dimension. This means that the burden of implementing this great task is put solely on the shoulders of man. Not heeding the warnings of two world wars, of Auschwitz and the Gulag, man is regarded as essentially good. The power of infinite creativity is attributed to his faith. Even the "spirituality for combat" does not really restore the divine dimension, for an analysis shows that the concept of spirituality is a merely anthropological category with syncretistic leanings.

The ecumenical one-world utopia is based on a monistic universalism. It does not take into consideration the forces of radical evil which are effective in this world and which poison every human attempt at progress. It ignores the biblical warning that the present antagonism between God and the Devil will lead to a disastrous climax for world history.

Our short analysis of the ecumenical vision has shown that it builds on ideological premises which are completely unacceptable to biblical thinking. We shall not be able to accept the ecumenical invitation. Rather, we are commissioned now to reexamine the testimony of biblical revelation in order to give an authentic evangelical response to the futuristic aspirations of modern man.

PART II: THE BIBLICAL WITNESS OF THE COMING KINGDOM

According to the testimony of the Holy Scripture, the Kingdom of God is an eschatological reality. This insight is decisive for our present theme, which tries to explore the relationship between history and eschatology. In the OT we meet the Kingdom essentially as an object of prophetic promises, in the NT as a fulfilled reality which, however, still has a dramatic history and a grand future.

The Kingdom as a Promise

That Jahweh as the only God always is and always has been the King of all creation and of the world of nations is the basic creed of Israel. In this dominion he is still going to win a great eschatological triumph over all ungodly and harmful forces. Such was the message of the prophets by which they dynamically reinforced faltering faith in times of national and religious crisis (see e.g., Isa 2:2ff.). God will wash away all sins; he will give new hearts to his people and pour out his Spirit upon all flesh. Then from the Mount of Zion his worldwide Kingdom of peace will be established. This glowing expectation was indeed the peculiar mark of Israel's faith in her election history. Here Bloch and the messianic Marxists have made an observation which from the viewpoint of the history of ideas and of religious psychology is correct.

Yet the biblical testimony and its modern interpretation are separated by a wide gulf. Biblical Messianism is not an ideology which proposes a historical goal to man and an active program to be worked out by himself. On the contrary, it is founded on the announcement of a series of extraordinary acts of God which supersede all human expectations and abilities. He is going to interfere from outside and from above in earthly history. "The Lord will fight for you, and you have only to be still" (Exod 14:14). This assurance holds true for all acts of salvation of which the Bible speaks. Therefore, that day, the date of which cannot be determined by man, is called the Day of the Lord. It is the day on which he will assemble all the nations for the execution of his judgment and for manifesting his rule over all the world. It comprises the totality of all deeds by which God himself at the end will establish the new world order.

This theocentric, eschatological view was preserved by Israel on through the inter-testamental period, as can be shown by the study of the different Messianic schools of thought.

When we proceed to the NT, we make a double observation. The NT confirms the promises of the Kingdom given by the prophets, but it changes their features as they are being fulfilled. It *confirms* the promise that God will manifest his dominion over his creation. The Kingdom is not wholly ethicized or spiritualized. But the implication of the promises begins with the soteriological concentration on the restoration of the broken relationship with God. This is the necessary precondition for the visible establishment of the Kingdom. Its coming, therefore, is implemented by two separate acts of God, which Karl Heim distinguishes as "world reconciliation" and "world consummation."[35]

The Kingdom Which Has Come in Jesus

The NT neither simply repeats nor negates the OT promises. Rather, it proclaims their fundamental realization in a surprising new form.

All Christ-events are fulfillments of eschatological promises. At the birth of Jesus, the heavens are opened and angels proclaim peace on earth. In his Sermon on the Mount he proclaims the divine Law of the messianic Kingdom. In his miracles the forces of the Kingdom expel the demons from their usurped positions. On the cross the decisive act of salvation is performed: Jesus offers himself as the expiating sacrifice for reconciling the world to God—the dividing wall between God and world, between heaven and earth, is broken down. "God was in Christ reconciling the world to himself" (2 Cor 5:18f.). The broken connection between God, who is the fountain of incorruptible life, and the world, which, separated from him, is delivered up to the forces of death, has been reestablished. Now there is hope once more for the first creation, hope that is revealed on the third day. For the resurrection of Jesus is the bridgehead of the new creation which enters and transforms the old one. Here is a visible assurance of the coming glory of God's Kingdom.

Garaudy openly declares (and it is hard not to feel that some of his ecumenical colleagues are in secret agreement) that the resurrection is simply a postulate of revolutionary hope, a challenge to change the world, which faith is unable to achieve. But the resurrection is not an imperative; it is a pure, incomprehensible gospel fact. God has intervened in the course of history. By raising his Son from the dead, God has already changed the course of the world from within. The objectivity of the resurrection of Jesus is of cardinal significance to the NT. For it is the foundation of our hope that all further promises, too, will be fulfilled at the final consummation. "By his great mercy we have been born anew to a living hope through the resurrection of Jesus Christ from the dead, and to an inheritance which is imperishable, undefiled, and unfading, kept in heaven for you, who by God's power are guarded through faith for a salvation ready to be revealed in the last time" (1 Pet 1:3-5).

The resurrection of Jesus is far more than an event which concerns his own destiny. From the resurrected Christ emanates the power of life eternal. Through the mystical communion with him which is constituted by our baptism into his death (Rom 6:3-5), the power of his resurrection gives new life to us also and the assurance of our likeness with him in our own resurrection.

The epistle to the Hebrews speaks of Christians as those "who have tasted the . . . powers of the age to come" (6:5). The ushering in of the eschatological Kingdom by the Christ event is crowned by his ascension. This means his enthronement on the right hand of God the Father, and the taking over of the royal rule over all powers in heaven and on earth. From now on the uplifted Christ sovereignly directs the course of history towards its victorious completion. On the Day of Pentecost he fulfills another important eschatological promise (Joel 3) by sending the gift of the Holy Spirit to his disciples. This establishes the communion between Christ as the Head and the Church as his body that empowers her to continue his own saving ministry on earth.

By communion with him, we live already now in the eschatological realm of his divine rule. This makes the church his "Kingdom of grace," as the early Protestant dogmaticians rightly called her. It is destined one day at the consummation of all things to be transformed into his "Kingdom of glory." Nourished by the Holy Spirit and purified by the test of affliction, Christian hope is able to transcend the horizon of our old world and be assured of the glory of the age to come.

The Kingdom in Its Coming Form of Glory

So far we have looked at the inner side of the fulfillment of the messianic prophecies (cf. Jer 31:31; Ezek 36:26f.). What is still lacking is the manifestation of the external side of the Kingdom. The peace of conscience, given by justification (Rom 5:1), is not yet complemented by visible social and political peace. Nations still engage in warfare and revolt against God. Satan still battles to retain his usurped positions. The realm of nature is not renewed yet. Together with the rest of creation, we still groan under our bodies' "bondage to decay" (Rom 8:21) and suffer under affliction, pain and death. That even this fate will be overcome one day is an important aspect of the OT promise of the Kingdom which is confirmed in the NT. This means that the Kingdom which has already arrived in Jesus still has a real future after his enthronement as Lord over heaven and earth. This future is the content of hope in its NT form. The designation of Jesus to be the Christ inseparably ties up the messianic Kingdom with him. Therefore, the NT hope for the coming of the Kingdom in glory (Matt 24:30; 25:31) is hope for the *parousia* of Jesus, the Son of Man. "Our Lord will come again" ("Maranatha"—1 Cor 16:22) is the core of Christian hope for the future. Here, too, the ancient prophecies of the coming Kingdom,

especially as shown by Daniel (7:13), find a Christological transformation.

Jesus Christ will come again with all his angels in great power
and glory and reveal himself visibly before the whole world. At the
end, every tongue will have to confess that the rule of the universe
is really his.

After the completion of world evangelization (Matt 24:14),
Jesus will take his now fully gathered congregation out of her eschatological warfare. He will unite her, together with those who have
already completed their earthly life, to himself. They will receive
eternal bliss and also a share in his eternal rule.

During Israel's confrontation with the hostility of the nations
in the final world war of this present age, Jesus will manifest himself as the Savior of God's first elected people. The Jews will "look
on him whom they have pierced" and turn to him as their Messiah
in deep contrition and faith (Zech 12:2-3, 9-10; Rom 11:26-28).
The conversion of Israel to Christ is a decisive condition for the
implementation of the holistic aspects of the eschatological reign of
God as visualized by the prophets. This condition is, however, overlooked by most theologians—both ecumenical and evangelical—
who presently deal with the biblical doctrine of the Kingdom. It was
left out both in Melbourne 1980 and Pattaya 1980 and in San
Antonio 1989. Moreover, it was not really stated in the prophetical perspective in Manila in 1989.[36]

Jesus will smite his apocalyptic opponent, the Antichrist, who
will be the embodiment of mankind's demonic rebellion. Finally he
will also deliver the Devil up to eternal punishment. Now the primal rebellion and the historic antagonism which originated from it
will be overcome forever.

All the dead will rise, and Christ will exercise judgment over
all mankind. The harvest of world history with all its deeds and
crimes will be manifested in its eternal significance. God's justice,
which has so often been veiled, will be made manifest before all generations. Man will have to account for every word and deed and
receive his righteous retribution.

Now the stage has been set for the final victory in the history of Christ's messianic conquests (1 Cor 15:24-26). Death will be destroyed. The first creation—i.e., the whole cosmos—will pass away. A new heaven and a new earth will be the scene of God's Kingdom in glory. The city of God will be with man, and the partition between transcendence and immanence will be removed. "Christ will deliver the Kingdom to God the Father . . . that God may be everything to everyone" (1 Cor 15:24, 28). I.e., the whole creation will then be liberated from hostility and decay and will be in perfect harmony with the aims of the Creator. The whole transfigured nature will then reflect the glory of God without distortion or defilement. It will be penetrated by God's own eternal being and will participate in his holiness, beauty and beatitude.

Eternity will not consist of a fellowship of disembodied spirits. It is true that our present world is separated from the future one by an abyss of cosmic cataclysm. But still, the new creation will be in an ontic continuation of identity with the present one; this is the significance of the message of the resurrection of the dead. Our personal resurrection is corresponded to by the promised liberation of all creation from the bondage of decay to the glorious liberty of the children of God. This means that the whole groaning creation will be transfigured by the glory of eternity.

Here we find the relevance of the biblical promise of the Kingdom for the concerns, hopes and anxieties of our contemporary world. Mankind is not left with illusory consolations or human solutions ending in frustration. At the bottom of every human hope, and even of the cry of the wounded animal, there lies a promise by which God has bound himself to his creation for eternity, and which he himself will fulfill in his own way at the end.

Let us sum up: There is a vast essential difference between the biblical hope for the Kingdom and all contemporary philosophies and theologies of history which reinterpret it ideologically.

(1) The hope for the transformation of the fallen world has its foundation not in psychological projections of a "principle of hope" which is residing in man, but in the biblical promise of God which was realistically confirmed by Christ's resurrection from the dead.

(2) Its terminal target is not the unreachable "wandering horizon" of expectation, but the second coming of Jesus Christ.

(3) Its contents are not the "open future" which we have to work out ourselves positively or negatively. On the contrary, the goal of salvation history is determined, unchangeable and indestructible. It is the reality of the eternal Kingdom which is already hidden with God and which will be manifested on the day of the eschatological consummation of the world.

Therefore, the epistle to the Hebrews (6:19) describes the hope set before us as the "anchor of the soul" that enters into the inner shrine behind the curtain, where Jesus has gone as a forerunner on our behalf.

The Kingdom in the Tension Between Arrival and Expectation

The time between the atonement and the consummation of the world is, as we saw, an interim period in the history of salvation. Although this was not to be foreseen from the OT perspective, Jesus has predicted it in several of his parables. It is not true that on account of his unfulfilled *parousia* the Early Church was forced to change the doctrine of the Kingdom or even to abandon it. But the delay in the manifestation of Christ's glory constitutes a crucial problem in our Christian understanding of history. It is equally important to be mindful both of the conditions and of the meaning of present history qualified as interim.

What are the conditions of this interim in salvation history? According to NT affirmations, three realities are to be taken into account:

First, *Jesus is already the invisible Ruler over heaven and earth*. The course of history, although seemingly steered by secular forces, is firmly under his control and is made to serve his purposes.

But on earth this rule is recognized only by his Church—which is his expanding Kingdom in grace. The rest of mankind either does not know yet of Christ's kingship or disobeys it. Therefore, they are objects of evangelization.

Second, until the return of Christ, *Satan and his demonic forces still fight to retain their position of power over this world*, although the Devil has lost his rights upon fallen man already. He is "bound" (cf. Luke 11:21f.); i.e., he has to retreat wherever the victory of Christ is boldly proclaimed and obeyed. Therefore, Satan tries to separate the Church from her Lord by means of seduction (false prophets) and persecution.

Thus, this interval is the period of the struggle between the Kingdom of Christ, heading for final victory, and the kingdom of Satan, facing final destruction. Every nation in which the gospel proclamation has gained a Christian bridgehead is conquered in principle, and it will benefit from divine blessings according to its degree of obedience. Still, Satan remains powerful enough to construct new positions. Moreover, towards the end of this interim he will unfold new forces again (Matt 24:10-12) and inspire "the man of lawlessness" to unite mankind under his anti-Christian world dominion (2 Thess 2:3-12; Rev 13:5-8; 17:12-14). The ecumenical utopia of the coming world community of all nations, religions and ideologies must be evaluated against this background.

Third, during this interim period *God rules mankind, as he did before, through the governing authorities* (Rom 13:1-7). Theirs is the task, on the basis of the natural law, of caring for external peace, maintaining justice/welfare, and punishing evildoers. The governing authorities are representatives of God in the civic realm and must be honored as such by all, including Christians.

The institution of the State is an order of preservation. God has given it to mankind in order to prevent chaos and to extend the time for repentance. The civic order does not, however, belong to the order of salvation. Therefore, political changes have no redemptive value. Nor can the governing authorities permanently secure the survival of mankind. On the contrary, the accelerating and magnifying catastrophes in history and nature remind us that we are living in an expiring age without a future. This shows that the contemporary plans to secure the survival of mankind by a complete revolution of the present world order are both illusory and deceptive as to their true nature and destination.

What, then, is the meaning of this interim and of the eschatological delay caused by it? The answer is to be sought in words such as Matt 28:18f. ("All authority in heaven and on earth is given to me. Go therefore and make disciples of all nations . . .") and 1 Cor 15:25 ("For he must rule until he has put all enemies under his feet"). The period between the ascension of Christ and his return in glory is not for the *establishment* of the Kingdom on earth, but for *preparation* for its coming. This implies the spiritual conquest of that dominion which in virtue of his work of atonement is already his by divine right, but which *de facto* is still occupied by those "principalities and powers" that oppose his rule. Karl Heim rightly taught that while the question of guilt has been answered at the cross, the question of power is still to be answered.

But this is not the only function of Christ's second coming. His *parousia* qualifies—although in a hidden way—the whole interim period. Our time is related to the coming Kingdom in several aspects. In it we are to give proof of our discipleship and Christian hope in a threefold way:

First, during the present period *the Church is to proclaim the Kingship of Christ and his salvation amongst all nations*. Only when Satan's power structures have been spiritually broken by the establishment of a messianic bridgehead within each nation, and when the total body of Christ, the Church, has grown up to her full stature (Col 2:19), will the condition for Christ's delivering the Kingdom to God the Father have been fulfilled.

Offering salvation for eternal life, not physical survival, is therefore the given priority within the total ministry of the Church.

Second, this is also the time to *give proof of our Christian hope by being obedient followers of Christ*. Our obedience is to be practiced not only in the religious duties of prayer and evangelization, but also within all other fields of human vocation. This insight gives a deeper meaning to honest labor. It is not done merely as a way of making a living, an unavoidable duty. It is also a service rendered to Christ himself, and thereby it receives a consecration for eternity: "Whatever you do, in word or deed, do everything in the name of the Lord Jesus" (Col. 3:17). Christians are to be salt and light in the world, and to seek the best for the heavenly city. They present themselves as Christ's servants by unselfishly seeking their neighbors' well-being and by continuing in Christian love beyond where other people have finished their duty. They boldly oppose the forces of seduction and do not lose patience when all good attempts seem to have been wasted. Hoping for the coming Kingdom, they are assured that every really good deed will be remembered (Rev 14:13). Thus, by the courageous obedience and the winning love of Christians, the signs of the coming Kingdom can shine already within this passing world order and inflame the hope for the complete appearance of the heavenly city amongst men.

Finally, during this present tension between the opposing ages, *Christian hope is to be generated and tested by tribulation* (Rom 5:2-5; 8:31-39). Temptations and afflictions sift out the true followers of Jesus from the nominal ones. At the same time, God singles out that closer circle which shall be united to Christ in a more special way. Those who have overcome tribulation will be deemed worthy both to inherit eternal life and also to participate in the eschatological reign of Jesus Christ. "He who conquers and who keeps my words until the end, I shall give him power over the nations . . ." (Rev 2:26); "If we endure we shall also reign with him" (2 Tim 2:12). Those consoling promises, addressed to the early Christian martyrs, are given to inspire Christians in all generations to manifest their hope for the coming glory even in the midst of subtlest temptations and severest tribulations.

THE KINGDOM—CHRIST'S PROMISE TO THE POOR
The Theology of the Poor in Biblical Perspective

"Blessed are the poor in spirit for theirs is the Kingdom of heaven" (Matt 5:3).

INTRODUCTORY NOTE

Shortly after the former International Missionary Council (founded in 1921) was incorporated into the World Council of Churches at New Delhi in 1961, the ecumenical understanding of mission underwent an important transformation. This change was indeed so drastic that at the conclusion of the 8th World Missionary Conference at Bangkok in January 1973, Dr. Emilio Castro, then director of Geneva's Department of World Mission and Evangelism, could pronounce programmatically: "We are at the end of a missionary era and just at the beginning of world mission." To lay the foundation of such a new ecumenical movement for world mission and to thrash out a corresponding mission strategy was the task of the following CWME (Commission on World Mission and Evangelism) meeting, which took place in May 1980 in Melbourne, where about 650 participants from 290 member churches were assembled.

GOD AND THE POOR IN CONTEMPORARY ECUMENICAL THEOLOGY

Although the theme of the Melbourne conference—"Your Kingdom Come"—sounded quite traditional, the way in which it was approached and unfolded from the perspective of the poor was rather revolutionary. True enough, poverty as the key problem of the Third World had already been the main topic of ecumenical social ethics since the middle of the sixties, especially at the famous Geneva Conference on Church and Society in 1966. Almost instantaneously many adopted Lenin's "theory of imperialism," according to which poverty is mainly the consequence of western colonial nations exploiting the colored nations, a process which is perpetuated today by the capitalist world system of economics. It is strange to observe how readily the WCC accepted this hypothesis into its own worldview. For rather than doing justice to the complex reasons for world poverty, this theory simplifies the economic realities.

If some nations—including the Japanese and the Taiwanese— enjoy a relative state of welfare, this is first of all the fruit of their cultural endeavor and their energetic employment of their God-given talents. This positive fact is overlooked, as are the multitude of reasons that cause the social misery of other peoples: a climate prone to produce natural disasters, the population explosion, religious fatalism (e.g., emerging from the Hindu concept of *karma*), the inability and corruption of national leadership, and finally murderous tribal and regional conflicts. Some Third-World countries' opening for international trade—which they want!—brings additional problems, no doubt. When the prices for raw materials produced by them are fixed internationally, they become dependent on the commercial laws of the world market. This, indeed, is a fatal factor in their present dilemma, which definitely ought to be tackled by those bodies who through their international trading agreements influence the world economy.

But it is misleading to declare this factor to be the only cause for underdevelopment. How blinded are those who recommend Socialism as the only remedy and at the same time do not take notice of the destructive results of the enforced socialistic system on the once flourishing economy of countries such as Mozambique, Cuba or Poland! Moreover, the poorest peoples in the world today are the fifteen million refugees, 90 percent of whom have run away or were expelled from socialist states such as Vietnam, Cambodia, Ethiopia or Afghanistan. All these are hard facts that determine the destiny of nations for better or for worse. But they are not taken into consideration by the social analysis of Marxist economic materialism, which has been accepted by Geneva's most trusted advisers like a dogma.

The ecumenical option for this ideological theory took place, as stated, at the Geneva Conference for Church and Society in 1966. There it also received a scanty and short-lived spiritual draping by the so-called Theology of Revolution. In Latin America especially, Roman Catholic authors sublimized this into the Theology of Liberation. Here, too, the biblical foundation remained rather weak, which impeded its reception by conservative churches.

To make up for this deficit, a new school of thought amongst European and American theologians emerged, developing the idea and practice of "Materialistic Bible Reading."[1] This venture was pioneered by three theologians working in France: Fernando Belo, Michel Clévenot, and George Casalis. In 1974 Belo published his commentary *Materialistic Reading of Mark's Gospel* (in French). Thereby he inaugurated a movement which soon crossed the borders of France and which now is growing in many countries. Belo formulated guiding questions for his new view of the Bible. How do the economic, political and ideological class struggles determine the production and reception of biblical texts? Which materialistic preconditions, interests and needs are leading to which terms, ideas and theories? Obviously, by such criteria Belo took his stand determinately with a Marxist philosophy of history.

In Germany this theological program was adopted and developed by NT scholar Wolfgang Stegemann and OT scholars Willy and Luise Schottroff, who are establishing their own school of materialistic, socio-historical Bible interpretation. Dorothee Sölle, too, has joined this group. According to Stegemann and L. Schottroff, almost nothing can be said with certainty about the person of Jesus, about his works and words. Only his crucifixion is an established fact. This particular way of execution shows that in the eyes of the Roman authorities he must have been a subversive political leader, and this indeed was his potential effect upon his followers. Since to the authors the person of Jesus is historically veiled, they prefer to speak of a "Jesus movement" which arose among the marginalized groups—impoverished and criminalized people—tax collectors, sinners, harlots, beggars, dispossessed, and cripples. This Jesus movement, they claim, was inspired by the idea that soon a complete turnover of all historical conditions would take place by which they, the poor, would become rulers in the Kingdom of God, which was about to be established by revolutionary events in which God himself was at work.

On the European continent, cells of Christian students were formed at universities and high schools for reading the Bible from a materialistic point of view, placing it side by side with the study of the writings of Marx and Lenin. The worldwide movement "Christians for Socialism" soon proved to be of tremendous significance for coordinating these groups. This movement, in its endeavor to promote Materialistic Bible Reading, is united by a threefold thrust.

First, they want to prove that the poor are the real subjects of the Bible.

Second, they want to wrest the Bible out of the hands of those who illegitimately have taken it into their possession and who have enchained it by their idealistic expository methodology, which, they feel, was developed by western theologians and church leaders in order to justify the established structures of domination.

Third, they want to read the Bible in such a way that by its light our political practice appears in a new clarity. Seen from the other side, our revolutionary engagement today will enable us to recognize undiscovered models of subversive strategies in the biblical records. One typical example which has been spread all over the world by ecumenical meetings is the reinterpretation of Mary's doxology, the Magnificat in Luke 1:46-56. This has now become the manifesto of social overthrow ("He has put down the mighty from their thrones") and also for women's liberation.

The principles of Materialistic Bible Reading have clearly left their marks on the documents of the World Mission Conference at Melbourne 1980. The reports of sections I, II and IV, which all have a socio-critical orientation, especially represent the person, preaching and works of Jesus exactly in accordance with that picture which the materialistic Bible exegetes have developed from what they claim to be the "oldest Jesus tradition." In the introduction to the report of section I the fundamental affirmation is quickly made:[2]

> God's judgement is revealed as an overturning of the values and structures of this world. In the perspective of the kingdom, God has a preference for the poor.

This preference for the poor is said to have been documented in the OT and confirmed by Jesus. The report continues:

> God identified with the poor and oppressed by sending his Son Jesus to live and serve as a Galilean speaking directly to the common people . . . and finally meeting death on a cross as a political offender.

In the same report we find the fundamental definition of poverty which the conference arrived at: "Poverty in the Scriptures is affliction, deprivation and oppression."

In the light of the presuppositions of the Theology of the Poor which we have noted above, we also understand the following statement: "The poor are 'blessed' because of their longing for justice and peace and their hope for liberation."[3] In their liberation— in the sociopolitical meaning—the poor themselves are decisively engaged. As the report goes on to explain: "The judgement of God . . . enables the poor to struggle to overthrow the powers that bind them. . . ." And only after such overthrow will it be "possible for both the humbled rich and the poor to become human, capable of response to the challenge of the kingdom."

At Melbourne the complete extreme in reinterpreting the Christian faith from the revolutionary perspective of the poor was exhibited by Julia Esquivel,[4] a former lay leader in Guatemala, where she had been organizing courses in Materialistic (sometimes also called "contextual") Bible Reading.

Contrasting two opposing forms of religiosity—evangelical quietism and the new spirituality which goes together with involvement in the freedom struggle—she identifies two images of God. The former "God" is the one whose image she had received through her own evangelical education. In the light of her recent political experiences "God" degenerates into a caricature of a political tyrant like Nicaragua's Somoza or the Shah of Iran. The other "unknown God" is manifested in the organized insurrection of the masses. He wears the features of the oppressed worker, who now stands upright and marches into the "kingdom of Life." This God is identified so closely with the revolutionary enthusiasm of the people's rebellion that Esquivel bestows upon him the names of honor of the triadic battle cry of the French Revolution.[5]

> He can only reign through a people, in a people that transforms itself, its paths, its life, its history and its future. That is the Justice-God, the Fraternal-God, the Liberation-God who appears also to us in the Exodus of the people of Israel and in each exodus of the people of the earth that march full of faith towards the kingdom of Life.

It is not our intention to pass judgment on the high degree of theological confusion which is exhibited here by a person whose subjective intention certainly is quite genuine. Even less will this aberration of her socio-ethical compassion induce us to be deaf to the sufferings of oppressed peoples in Latin America and elsewhere described by Julia Esquivel. The point which we really want to make is that the understanding of the poor which is exposed here is the central concept of the new ecumenical theology of mission which was developed in Melbourne. Esquivel's inflammatory speech was not simply a personal statement of an outsider; it was ordered by the organizers who planned that conference in their WCC Geneva headquarters.

The poor were described in Melbourne as the "sinned against," while their own distorted relation with God did not come into focus. Rather they were seen as those who through their own struggle win their redemption. The Kingdom of God becomes so wholly secularized that Esquivel without hesitation can transform the biblical phrase "a new heaven and a new earth" (Rev 21:1) into her own formula: "a new earth and a new society." It is that kingdom which the poor are creating for themselves in virtue of their spiritual "resurrection"—i.e., their insurrection.

Here we encounter an apotheosis of the poor that goes hand in hand with the abandonment of the traditional understanding of God and his Christ. By their total identification with "God the worker" and "Christ the labourer," the poor are elevated into the position of those who are acting alone and who are capable of their own resurrection to arrive at the "kingdom of Life." The only condition is that they believe in it: they must become conscious of their own power and join their forces in a fellowship of solidarity.

Is it still necessary to point out the analogy between this "theological" concept of the poor and the salvific role which Karl Marx ascribes to the proletariat as the subject of revolution?

BIBLICAL EVALUATION

Having noted in which ideological way the poor were spoken of at the Melbourne conference, we must now reevaluate the biblical evidence.

Both Testaments do, indeed, display much concern for the poor. This becomes evident by the frequent occurrence of poverty terminology. The early writings of the OT clearly imply that the God of Israel wants all of his people to enjoy a genuine fellowship in which they can develop their lives. Reminding the Israelites of their vital community during their forty years in the desert, they are admonished not to permit any oppressive relationship such as slavery amongst them, since they are called brothers. If somebody sells himself into serfdom to a fellow Hebrew, he shall go free after six years for nothing (Exod 21:2). In the year when the field lies fallow, that which grows shall be reaped and eaten by the poor. Jahweh, the God of Israel, forbids the perversion of justice due to the poor (Exod 23:6). He is the compassionate protector of the poor (22:27), a feature which is stressed over and over in Israel's entire history. Many of the dooming prophecies, especially by Amos and Isaiah, are calls for repentance to the mighty and rich to cease oppressing the poor and to restore justice to widows and orphans. Those who do not heed are severing their ties with God, and he rejects their prayers and sacrifices (cf. Amos 2:6-7; 4:1, 5, 7; Isa 1:15-17; 9:12-16; Jer 5:3-5).

It is of decisive significance that in such calamity the poor man's *relationship with God* comes into focus. Finding no human support, no righteous judge who restores his right and lifts up the downtrodden, the poor man turns to the Lord as his protector. From here the Hebrew word *anij* ("the poor") increasingly receives a religious connotation.

Inasmuch as a person who really is an *anij* of Jahweh trustfully turns to him, *anij* becomes a synonym for humble or pious (Ps 18:28).[6] Particularly in the later Psalms the *anijim* are presented as people who humbly put their confidence in God's intervention. Less and less does the expression "to be poor" refer to a person's being economically disadvantaged, but rather now means to turn to God with humble petition in all one's sufferings and needs.

On the other hand, the OT wisdom literature also expresses the insight that social poverty may be caused by one's own inertia, and consequently the poor are sometimes reproached (cf. Prov 6:6-11).

It is important to observe that Israel always interpreted her misfortune within the framework of her covenant relationship and understood it as an evil permitted or directly sent by God himself. This applies to all disasters in the realm of history or nature. This was the vital message of the prophets (Amos 3:6). National catastrophes were punishments inflicted by God on his people because they had broken his law and thus had broken the covenant. Inasmuch as the conscience is refined and awareness of sinfulness grows, man comes to understand that he is never righteous in the eyes of God. Rather, he has to pray for forgiveness and live by God's grace. Through his redemptory pedagogy in the OT, by his punishing and by his restoration, God intends to show Israel her complete and exclusive dependence on him. In this sense the expression "the poor" finally becomes a technical term in rabbinic literature, referring to the entire people of Israel. If the people in repentance put their whole confidence in the Lord, he will manifest himself as the One who is faithful to his covenant, as the One who is merciful.

Although the prophets had repeatedly exhorted Israel to repent, such a humble and obedient attitude towards God was never shown by the totality of the people in its history, but only by certain humble and pious individuals, the *anijim*. Therefore, the expression "the poor" came to receive an eschatological connotation. Zephaniah announces a terrible judgment which the Lord will afflict upon the world of nations for their purification. In this connection the Lord through Zephaniah prophesies to Israel: ". . . you shall no longer be haughty in my holy mountain. For I will leave in the midst of you a people humble and lowly. They shall seek refuge in the name of the Lord, those who are left in Israel . . . they shall pasture and lie down, and none shall make them afraid" (3:11-13). Thus, it becomes more and more the concern of the eschatologically-oriented pious to belong to those "humble [or poor] and lowly."

At the time of Jesus there existed a religious movement with several facets which called itself the *anawim* (Aramaic form). They were motivated by the expectation that the prophecies of salvation for Israel would soon be fulfilled. It is worth noting that in Israel there has never existed a political party of poor people who tried to use violence for getting their social claims fulfilled.

In his messianic mission, Jesus expressly addressed himself to the poor, as was pointed out correctly at Melbourne. His preaching of the gospel to the poor is emphasized in the summaries of his messianic work (Luke 4:18; 7:22). Out of this indisputable evidence a threefold exegetical question arises:

> (1) Who are the poor?
> (2) Why does Jesus turn just to them?
> (3) What is the content of the gospel which he preaches to the poor? Or, What is the nature of the Kingdom of God which he promises to them?

Who Are "the Poor"?

In their versions of the first Beatitude, Luke simply mentions "the poor," whereas Matthew adds the qualification "in spirit." By this Matthew wanted to communicate to his readers the connotation with which biblically educated listeners would hear this term anyway. The promise of salvation made by Jesus is fulfilled in those who do not insist upon their own claims, who do not rely on their own strength, piety or wealth (which alas! the rich mostly do; cf. Luke 16:19-31; Matt 13:22), but who rather approach God in humility, repentance and faith, being wholly aware of their unworthiness and helplessness. Such an attitude is more likely to be found amongst those who are in material want, although not automatically. In other words, nobody is accepted simply on account of social poverty, and nobody is excluded simply because of economic wealth. Acceptance and rejection are determined by the inner attitude connected with it.

Why Does Jesus Turn Only to "the Poor"?

John the Baptist and Jesus himself preached that only those who have given evidence of true repentance will be accepted into the impending Kingdom of Heaven. For others, the coming of the Kingdom will mean judgment and condemnation. The teaching of the Beatitudes must be understood in this light. The phrase "the poor in spirit" can be taken as an exact analogy to Paul's doctrine of justification: because of Christ's atoning self-sacrifice, God justifies and bestows his peace upon those who receive this offer of grace by faith without boasting in their good works of the Law. The terms used by Jesus and Paul differ, but the theological implication is the same.

What Is the Nature of the Promised Kingdom?

In preaching the good tidings of the Kingdom, Jesus revitalized the content of hope which the pious in Israel had cherished and still were cherishing. The novelty was that he now authoritatively announced the immediate fulfillment of that expectation which the poor in spirit always had held with great longing. The fulfillment is described formally by the term "gospel," while the term "Kingdom of God" states its content. The fulfillment came in Jesus' own messianic mission to his people. He is the anointed messenger mentioned in Isa 6:1-2. He is the One in whom the Kingdom of God has arrived. This is manifested by his messianic signs.

According to the ecumenical Theology of the Poor, and according to the proponents of "Materialistic Bible Reading," the Kingdom preached by Jesus to the poor is the beginning of a new state of affairs, an age of prosperity, a reversal of the existing order. Those who formerly had been poor and marginalized will now enjoy welfare, social liberty, and a share in the political rule. Such expectation surely was in the minds of many of Christ's first listeners, probably even of his own disciples. This is why they became so disappointed by the real behavior of Jesus, which contradicted such imagination, and why they despaired at the exit event of his earthly career. True enough, particularly in the beginning of his ministry, Jesus did perform many miracles which corresponded with the expected spiritual and physical *shalom* of the messianic age. But they were *semeia*, signs pointing forward. He performed them to arouse and to confirm the belief that he was the Messiah, the Son of God, the Son of David, and the apocalyptical Son of man who was to stand in the center of the promised Kingdom of God. But the divine rule which he was restoring on earth was still restrained to the preliminary stage of mystery (Matt 13:11). The cosmic turnover which was predicted by the OT prophets did not occur.

Whenever his fellow Israelites or even his own disciples pressed him to introduce this final stage, he withdrew from them (John 6:15).

The messianic deeds which Luke enumerates in 4:18-19 and 7:22-33 are not to be interpreted in the literal sense, as many ecumenical expositors are inclined to do, for if this were the case, Jesus would have liberated John the Baptist and all those similarly imprisoned from their chains. What really is meant is the release of those imprisoned under the bondage of sin and demons. The coming of the Kingdom in power and glory remained still a future event, which Jesus clearly distinguished from the present stage of the Kingdom which he had already initiated. On certain occasions he also indicated there was still a very important precondition to be fulfilled before the final state could be realized: the gospel of the Kingdom had to be proclaimed to all nations (Matt 24:14; Mark 13:10).

What Jesus by his message is offering at once to the poor in spirit is their participation in his Kingdom in its preliminary form. This means their newly restored relationship as children of God the Father in virtue of his Holy Spirit bestowed upon them, redemption from their spiritual fetters, and fellowship with Jesus and his followers. At the same time it means their candidacy for participation in the coming Kingdom in its eschatological fullness, if they trust in him and remain faithful followers on the road to the cross. In the present time the followers of Jesus remain *anawim*, people who are poor in spirit, humble, repentant, confident, who expect their redemption in its completeness only from God's eschatological intervention. This will take place when the Son of man comes on the clouds of heaven with power and great glory (Matt 24:30), when he will send his angels to gather his elect from the four winds, in order to give to them the Kingdom prepared for them as their heritage from the foundation of the world (Matt 25:34).

In the light of this biblical evidence, nothing is more devious than the attempt to read from Christ's blessing of the poor an agitated summons to the politically and socially oppressed that they, under the leadership of Jesus, should take their destiny into their own hands, cast off their chains, and snatch from the rich their possessions in order to divide them amongst themselves. This would be the absolute opposite to that attitude of *anijim* which Jesus expected from his followers. The coming Kingdom of God has nothing to do with a new political and economic world order which must be achieved by engagement in class struggles. Jesus never promised that during the course of the present age the problem of poverty would be settled. On the contrary, when he perceived an ideology of the poor in the words of his own disciples, he emphasized, "For you have the poor always with you" (Mark 14:7).

The reason for this sobering clarification was that Jesus did not find the root cause of poverty in a wrong economic order which could be corrected by introducing another system of economy. Rather, he perceived it as the consequence of human sin, *which will be eradicated neither from the rich nor from the poor during this aeon*, but which on the contrary will come to a final universal outburst at its end (Matt 24:7). This excludes any utopia of a classless society without poor here on earth. This does not mean that the Church of Jesus Christ and its members should simply acquiesce in the face of world poverty or remain unmoved by the misery of the world's poor. Neither does it mean that the Church—in contrast to the OT prophets—should simply remain silent about the exploitation of suppressed people by tyrannical rulers and selfish rich (cf. Jas 5:1-5). The Church must exercise her critical influence but only in the power of the Spirit, as the prophets too have done. The Church is neither commissioned nor permitted to employ violence to enforce her social claims. The contribution of the Church in alleviating the needs of the poor consists mainly in realizing her own brotherly communion, in mercifully ministering to the suffering, in teaching the norms which God has set for a harmonious human fellowship, and in unfeigned readiness to open her mouth on behalf of those who suffer unjustly.

CHAPTER FIVE

THE IDEOLOGICAL TRANSFORMATION OF THE KINGDOM AT MELBOURNE 1980

*T*he 10th International Missionary Conference at Melbourne, sponsored by the WCC's Commission on World Mission and Evangelism (CWME), was the first in that ecumenical series of meetings for which a biblical theme had been chosen, the second petition of the Lord's Prayer—"Your Kingdom Come." The sponsors were aware, no doubt, that both in the OT and NT the Kingdom of God is the central content of biblical hope and thus has an eschatological nature. Thus the Kingdom was reflected upon on the basis of a prayer for its coming. In the Preparatory Document drafted in Geneva, the selection of this petition is motivated by the remark:

> It obliges us to consider the realms of nature and history, and provides a clear eschatological perspective.[1]

The deliberations at the conference itself were marked by the guiding view that hope for the Kingdom initiates a dramatic course of events that will conclude in its appearance. In the documents the center of these events is not seen in the ingathering of believers into the messianic community, the Church, but rather in the humanization of the secular society. Three of the four section reports show an obvious tendency to discard the ecclesiologically determined *salvation history* in favor of a universal history of mankind in which salvation is realized progressively by liberating actions in the field of repressive social structures. These views are essential tenets of Process Theology which one can discover in various shades of ecumenical reflections on history. This leads us to the crucial question pertaining to the Melbourne theme: What is the relation between the Kingdom of God as it is realized already within our present history and its full appearance at the end of history? Amongst the "disputed questions" listed in the Preparatory Document this very problem is stated with the following words:

> Is it possible to see the world's events as parts and phases of an overall dynamic process towards the kingdom?[2]

This question, true enough, is to be directed to any theological unfolding of the Kingdom message. For the NT maintains, on the one hand, that in the historical coming of Jesus of Nazareth the Kingdom which had been predicted by the prophets has already appeared. On the other hand, the NT writings also proclaim the future of the Kingdom that will appear in power and glory when Jesus Christ will come again with all his angels and chosen saints (cf. Matt 24:30f.).

The Church in her doctrine has attempted to give justice to these twofold biblical statements by terminologically discerning between God's *Kingdom in grace* and his *Kingdom in glory*. These two are kept apart by a clear apocalyptical intervention: the cataclysmic end of this old aeon, which is dominated by the prince of this world, and the return of Jesus Christ, which ushers in the resurrection of the dead. Thus, the element of hope in the Kingdom was safeguarded as a foretaste of coming fulfillment side by side with a full appreciation of its spiritual blessings which can be experienced and mediated by the Church now.

Glimpses of this traditional view can be discovered in the Melbourne documents, too, especially in the Report of Section III, "The Church Proclaims the Kingdom," which had attracted the majority of evangelical and Orthodox participants. Here we read in its preamble the important statement which obviously reveals a Catholic or Orthodox authorship.

> The whole church of God, in every place and time, is a sacrament
> of the kingdom which came in the person of Jesus Christ and will
> come in its fulness when he returns in glory.[3]

The Church, so one can conclude, mediates the grace of the coming Kingdom in a sacramental way, but, according to the following paragraphs, also through its preaching, its diaconate, and its loving fellowship. The Kingdom will appear in its fullness when Jesus Christ returns in his glory.

But not even this conservative section took the trouble to explore more deeply the eschatological problem which is implied in this biblical insight, for it induces us to go on by asking: Why does the Kingdom wear such preliminary shape now, and what are the preconditions for its visual appearance in its completed form? These questions could only be clarified by a careful consideration of biblical salvation history, which was, however, impeded by the theological pluralism amongst the participants even of this section. Otherwise they ought to have clarified by what kind of *powers* the coming of the Kingdom is still being delayed. They ought to have talked about the particular eschatological calling of the *Church*, which first has to be collected out of all nations by the worldwide witness to the gospel of the Kingdom.

Another important aspect of NT prophecy is the salvific future of God's ancient covenant people *Israel* (Romans 11), which, however, is never mentioned in any Melbourne document!

In contrast to the at least rudimentary biblical view of Section III, we encounter in the remaining bulk of the conference report a rather heterogeneous view, although it is never unfolded systematically. Its clearest presentation was given in the keynote addresses delivered by Dr. Emilio Castro (then director of CWME) and the Syrian-Orthodox Metropolitan from South India, the Most Rev. Mar Osthathios. The reports of Sections I, II and IV reveal this current ecumenical view only in occasional statements of more principal theological nature. But their ambiguous usage of biblical terms, closely intertwined with ideological concepts, tends to obscure their real implications.

In this secular-ecumenical theology the futurist nature of God's Kingdom is maintained too. In this way the abiding superiority of its expectation is emphasized over against all preliminary and anticipating sociopolitical projects.

In a further step, the WCC theologians try to underline the futurist nature of the Kingdom by employing the term *utopy*, which is a key word in many ecumenical documents, mostly used interchangingly with its synonym, *vision*. Facing the absolute shape of the Kingdom, they appoint far-ranging goals for human action— including the churches' mission—whose norms correspond with this utopic vision as closely as possible. Referring to the biblical passages of Isa 65:17-25 and Revelation 21—22, the Geneva Preparatory Document for Melbourne states:

> These visions and expressions of hope are *absolute utopias* that express in symbols the will and promise of God for total justice, renewal, recreation, healing, peace and reconciliation that transcend every historical situation. They provide an illustration of what it means when we pray "Your Kingdom come, your will be done" and a framework for imagining or identifying *relative or concrete utopias* that are operative in the actual socio-economic situation of the world. Thus, Christians who today feel the necessity for discovering new historical embodiments of God's call to liberation, peace and reconciliation, to "seek first his kingdom and justice," can find criteria by which they will be able to participate in the common human search for a new and more just social order. In its recent programme emphasis on a *"Just, Participatory and Sustainable Society*," the World Council of Churches is attempting to imagine criteria and guidelines for this discernment.[4]

Besides this attempt of the WCC to develop its own global utopia for a coming world community, we also find ecumenical theologians who rather advocate the reception of a given ideological utopy. Often one chooses Marxism for orientation. Thus, in a preparatory consultation at the Ecumenical Institute at Bossey, near Geneva, in 1979, Dr. Enrique Dussel expounded the following thesis:

> In Latin America, for instance, between the present situation of oppression and dependence on North American capitalism and the final Kingdom beyond history is to be found the vision of a new system in history—e.g. the socialist one.[5]

While theoretically the distinction is maintained between the Kingdom of God in its final (probably never attainable) form and the utopic visions, the whole interest is attached to the latter. The utopias in which by human action the promised conditions of the coming Kingdom seem to have been implemented approximately constitute the criteria for the possibility of cooperating with other social movements which, directed by their own utopic visions, also are working for an ideal future state of humanity.

Now, as a matter of fact, the utopias of modern ideologies and innovation movements within other religions have indeed often been influenced by Christian prophecy. This is why ideological visions and Christian Kingdom expectation disclose so many similarities. On this account, it was concluded at Melbourne that Christians and non-Christians should join hands for a common mission and work for a common goal. Three decisive points were, however, overlooked in this synthesizing proposal:

First, it was overlooked that the biblical expectation of the Kingdom in its fullness is not based on human action but solely on God's apocalyptic intervention.

Second, it was overlooked that God's Kingdom cannot be established in the course of our present history, because it is resisted by the growing force of evil which will not be removed before this old aeon has run out. The encounter between the gospel of the

Kingdom with the forces of Satan results in a process of separation that finally will culminate in the confrontation with the world dominion of the Antichrist.

Third, the biblical view was blurred—namely, that the temporal blessings of God's Kingdom proceed from the power of forgiveness and from the renewal through the Holy Spirit which transforms persons from within. The ideological utopias, on the other hand, are to be realized by scientific analyses and political methods, and may even demand violent struggle.

The Melbourne documents give the general impression that at that mission conference a view of the coming Kingdom was prevailing in which its apocalyptical character is replaced by an ideological vision which is to be implemented within history by the conquests of liberation struggles. This impression is undergirded by nine observations:

(1) The transcendental character of the Kingdom is seen in Jesus' statement before Pilate: "My Kingdom is not of this world . . ." (John 18:36). That same character is emphasized in all apocalyptical descriptions of its miraculous irruption out of the heavenly world. In the Melbourne documents that transcendence recedes completely behind expositions in purely immanent categories. Numerous delegates may still have believed in the Kingdom of Heaven. That belief shines through in some formulations, especially in the hymnic conclusions of some reports. But nowhere does it constitute the point of gravitation when the real concerns are presented. And yet, how natural would it have been for a mission conference to point to the coming Kingdom in glory as the main incentive to stimulate the churches again for the evangelization of the world, just as this has been done throughout the course of the evangelical mission movement up to our present day!

(2) The conference's turning away from apocalyptical realism becomes even more apparent by its almost complete silence about the personal return of Christ as the bringer of the Kingdom. Only two times is it shortly mentioned in the report of Section III, but it is absent in the message of the conference, a theologically meager document anyway. When Ernst Käsemann, one of the main speak-

ers, was asked in a press conference why he had not mentioned the second coming of Christ, the Tübingen scholar reacted in fury, "I am not at all interested in that; Jesus is the Lord, that is enough for me!"[6]

(3) The Melbourne documents say nothing about the coming catastrophes and the *apocalyptical signs* which, according to biblical prophecy, will precede the return of Christ, especially the necessary witness unto all nations (Matt 24:14; Mark 13:10) and the gathering and conversion of Israel (Romans 11). Remarkably absent is any reference to the preceding appearance of Antichrist. Undoubtedly, it is omitted for the negative reason that this biblical warning is strident with the progressive optimism of the WCC's view on history.

(4) The Melbourne documents resound with a legalistically demanding tone. They put great weight upon churches' and Christians' actions as if the establishment of the Kingdom were completely dependent on them. "I experienced a disproportion between the demands of the Law and the power of the Gospel . . . in a climate with little spiritual life and Christian assurance," commented the Norwegian delegate Dr. Åge Holter in his "Report from Melbourne."[7]

(5) The Melbourne Report assigns eschatological dignity to what its authors regard as *signs of the Kingdom*. The coming Kingdom is consistently described in terms of ideal targets which are to be reached by political endeavors and are dependent on their success. This view pervades particularly the report of Section II, "The Kingdom of God and Human Struggle," as may be gathered from the following quotations:

> The World Council of Churches has expressed in various ways its solidarity with the struggles of liberation and has thus become a sign of the Kingdom of God to many people (II, 12).[8]

> Wherever a religion or its revival enhances human dignity, human rights and social justice for all people, and brings in liberation and peace for everybody, there God may be seen to be at work (II, 21).[9]

The eschatological visions of the New Testament and the life and teaching of Jesus himself show that the Kingdom of God is not unrelated to the building of a society which seeks equal opportunities for all (II, 25).[10]

It is true that sometimes it is said the "the Kingdom in its fullness" renders any human achievement "only approximate and relative" (Section I, 4). However, this formula seems to serve in the function of an absolute ideal, a "utopy" to prevent people from relaxing in their permanent quest for improvement.

(6) The biblical view of the eschatological reward for Christian martyrs is secularized, too, and is presented as a fruit which will be harvested as a result of the historical process of liberation. As Emilio Castro states of the assassination of Archbishop Romero of San Salvador:

His sacrifice and the sacrifice of the many other Salvadorians is fruitful not only for the historical destiny of the Salvadorian people, but also, in the total economy of the kingdom, for the working out of God's eternal plans to bring all things to newness in Jesus Christ.[11]

For sure, Castro made this statement in connection with his testimony to a Kingdom "that is not limited through the horizon of our historical death." But by similar words political movements have always commemorated the casualties in their battles as victims who have not died in vain. What they have in view is always the final victory of their vision, but not that Kingdom which Jesus will someday establish on an earth completely renewed by himself.

(7) The Kingdom of God as a future state hoped for appears to be the organic *completion of the work of human beings* rather than an eschatological act of God.

The Good News of the Kingdom will then be recognized as such, will become polemic, will invite us to enter into an historical struggle that culminates in the total transformation of creation.[12]

(8) The Kingdom hoped for at Melbourne betrays its secular nature also in the description of *concrete goals.* Metropolitan Osthathios infers from the prophetic vision of the messianic reign in Isaiah 2 the duty of Christians to ask their governments for disarmament, "changing swords into ploughshares." The following sentence shows how he envisages the implementation of such an appeal:

> Thinkers like Arnold J. Toynbee are showing the need of a world government, but the rich nations are diametrically opposed to it, for they are more concerned about maintaining their own living standard than the coming of the Kingdom of God in the whole world.[13]

The world government as asked for by Toynbee and other one-world ideologists is seen as the "coming of the Kingdom of God in the whole world"! The apprehension that such a world dominion erected by human planning might in reality prove to be the reign of the Antichrist does not strike the minds of this church leader and his listeners.

(9) Forgotten at Melbourne was the biblical message of the coming *extreme judgment.* This omission is serious, because it is here that the twofold exit of world history will show its ultimate consequences. But this scriptural teaching Osthathios discards by synthesizing the views of Karl Barth and Teilhard de Chardin into a universalism that—in the name of Christ!—does not even shun the danger of syncretism:

> As pointed out by Karl Barth and others, those who preach eternal hell preach it for others and not for themselves. Our lingering fear of syncretism is due to the lack of faith in the transforming Christ, the Logos at work in all religions and ideologies, and the "far-off Event to which the whole creation is moving; the Alpha and the Omega."[14]

Such discarding and manipulating of biblical truth must necessarily lead to a consistent perversion of the Kingdom of God as taught in Scripture.

The gospel of the Kingdom proclaims God as the One who by triumphing over all his enemies himself reestablishes his salvific dominion on earth. The goal of the history of God's reign according to the Bible is the glorification of God the Father and of his Son Jesus Christ:

> And I heard a loud voice in heaven, saying, "now the salvation and the power and the Kingdom of our God and the authority of his Christ have come . . ." (Rev 12:10).

> Then I heard what seemed to be the voice of a great multitude, like the sound of many waters and like the sound of mighty thunderpeals, crying, "Hallelujah! For the Lord our God the Almighty reigns. Let us rejoice and exult and give him the glory . . ." (Rev 19:6f.).

Where this theocentric and doxological orientation of the biblical Kingdom message is disregarded, where the perspective is directed not towards God but rather towards man as the beneficiary of the Kingdom, there it is perverted into an *ideology*. It becomes a secular gospel which nourishes itself from the visions of biblical prophecy and the language in which the saving events are related in the NT. But its point of departure is the immanent needs of *man*, whose spokesmen the adherents of the ideology claim to be. It drafts a plan of salvation to be implemented by man himself, and it raises human wishes to the dignity of ultimate concerns. *In the deepest analysis, we encounter the perversion of God's Kingdom into a Kingdom of Man.*

For the Church and her mission, such an undertaking exercises its greatest danger not where an ideology openly manifests itself in its anti-Christian character—as, e.g., in National-Socialism or in plain Marxism-Leninism. The danger becomes far greater when the ideological transformation subtly conceals itself under a theological cloak, where its proponent constantly invokes God or Christ or recites biblical affirmations, but silently reinterprets them in an anthropocentric way. In the history of the concept of God's Kingdom, such anthropocentric reinterpretations have emerged several times. To start with they appeared in a fanatical religious shape, as expounded, e.g., by Montanus in the third century or by Thomas Müntzer in sixteenth-century Germany. Since the age of the Enlightenment and the French Revolution, however, we encounter the reinterpreted Kingdom in a philosophical or ideological shape. We may think of the idealization of the "Kingdom of God" in Hegel's philosophy of history or of its materialistic turnover in the teaching of Karl Marx.

In modern ecumenism, such ideological reinterpretation assumes a pseudo-theological form. An analysis of the Melbourne documents could show that this was done persistently at the 9th World Missionary Conference, although not to the same degree in all addresses and section reports. It is astonishing that this ideological subversion of the Christian doctrine could remain almost unnoticed by most of the delegates at Melbourne, including theologians and church leaders. And it is equally astonishing that such transformation into an ecumenical ideology could be achieved within the framework of all confessional traditions. The most bewildering example was produced by the much acclaimed lecture of the Syrian-Orthodox Metropolitan Mar Osthathios, who made the hazardous experiment to base the concept of the classless society on the orthodox doctrines about the Holy Trinity and the divinization of the believer (*theiosis*).

It is possible to compose a whole glossary of central Christian concepts that in the Melbourne documents received a semantic reinterpretation:

The *Good News* brings the fulfillment of legitimate human expectations and dreams (Canaan Banana).

The *Kingdom of God* is approached in the socialist economic system (Section IV, 25).

The *gifts of the Kingdom* bring the satisfaction of the most elementary human needs.

Principalities and powers are the existing political and economic structures, especially the capitalist system and multinational concerns (*passim*).

Mission is the struggle of the Christian and his neighbors against the forces that sin against them (Raimund Fung).

Evangelization is the participation in the battle for a more just social order (Section IV, 19).

Easter is happening in the victory of the people of Nicaragua (Julia Esquivel).

Pentecost is the enablement to start again in the struggle for the transformation of all reality (Emilio Castro).

The heavenly Jerusalem is the ecologically sustainable city (Geneva Preparatory Document).

Parallel with such ideological transformation of the gospel, the WCC shows its increasing readiness to engage not only in dialogue but also in a relation of partnership with the ideologies. In his preview on Melbourne the CWME director E. Castro declared the ideologies to be important points of reference: "How does God act in history? What is the relationship between the religio-ideological systems of mankind and the Kingdom of God?" he asks. He answers his question himself:

> We live today in a pluralistic situation, side by side with people belonging to different religious persuasions or ideologies. In our daily life we give and we receive, we listen to the witness of other faiths and offer our own witness. In this living together, working together, sharing together, possibilities for shaping a better tomorrow are open to all of us.[15]

Among the ideological systems whose partnership was sought by the WCC at Melbourne, Marxism was allocated the primary position. At the preparatory consultation at Bossey in 1979 Enrique Dussel declared:

> The historical goal of socialist liberation is opposed to the ruling capitalist system and can—indeed must—be expounded in relation to the eschatological project of liberation in the Kingdom.[16]

In the eyes of the conference leadership, Communism held no deterring force. On the contrary, Metropolitan Mar Osthathios openly confessed in his lecture at Melbourne that he and four other Syrian Orthodox bishops—unlike their Roman Catholic colleagues—in a recent election in the South Indian federal state of Kerala had pleaded to vote for the Left in spite of its avowed atheism, "because the devil is no atheist (Jas 2:19), but an anti-humanist and an evil person." Osthathios even hoped to win Communism from within. He motivated his optimism by commenting:

> The atheism of communism cannot last too long and the materialism of capitalism is also likely to shift if the gospel of the kingdom is presented to both with the practice of a theology of classless society.[17]

The persistent ideological penetration of ecumenical thinking was completed in Melbourne by the consensus amongst the conference's participants to adopt the basic elements of the *Theology of Liberation*, provided that a variety of regional adaptations is conceded. Obviously they disregarded the warning that human history has witnessed many ideological movements—e.g., Leninism, National-Socialism, Maoism, Sandinism—wearing the slogan "Freedom" on their banners, which after their completed conquest immediately proceeded to enslave the liberated ones in order to ensure their "total liberation."

CHAPTER SIX

PEOPLE'S THEOLOGIES IN QUEST FOR A POLITICAL KINGDOM

PART I: THE FOUR SOURCES OF "PEOPLE'S THEOLOGY"

1. Third-World Theological Associations

When we trace the origin of the modern endeavor to stimulate popular theological creativity, we must first mention all those regional and continental associations of indigenous theologians in Asia, Africa and Latin America which came into existence after the Third Assembly of the World Council of Churches (WCC) in New Delhi in 1961. Attempts to develop an indigenous theology closely related to the traditional culture had been made for a long time in India, for instance, ever since the beginning of the last century. But in the era of decolonization, which began in the 1950s, the theological work of indigenous Christian thinkers came under the influence of nationalism and racial consciousness. In stressing their cultural autochthony and dissociating themselves from western tradition, they sought intellectual solidarity in newly established associations. Their original concern was an inculturation of Christianity. Examples of this are the several proposals for an "Indian

Theology," the so-called "African Theology," and the Japanese "Theology of the Pain of God" by K. Kitamori.

In other areas, however, theology is done to serve the interests of psychological and political liberation from western domination. This is true with regard to "Black Theology" in the USA and southern Africa, "Liberation Theology" in Latin America, the "Homeland Theology" in Taiwan, and the "Minjung Theology" in South Korea. There is an inner analogy between all these theologies, especially in their common inductive, socio-critical point of departure. This parallelism is not accidental. It is due to a mutual influence which has been encouraged or even planned by ecumenical agents, as can be shown by the origin and development of the Ecumenical Association of Third World Theologians (EATWoT). The first stage of EATWoT's history is described and documented in a volume edited by Sergio Torres and Virginia Fabella, entitled *The Emergent Gospel* (New York: Maryknoll, 1976).

Through the initiative of the Chilean protagonist of liberation theology, Sergio Torres, the first ecumenical conference of Third World Theologians was convened in Dar es Salaam in August 1976. Twenty-one representatives from Africa, Asia, Latin America, the Caribbean Islands and the North American black population attended. Some westerners sympathetic to political theology were invited as observers and promised to raise financial support.

> The participants agreed that the inherited Western theology was inadequate . . . and that a new model was needed. To achieve this, they resolved to establish an Ecumenical Association of Third World Theologians.[1]

Its purpose was to systematically develop contextual theologies and convene similar EATWoT meetings for each of the three continents of the Third World, in order to organize the participants into analogous regional ecumenical associations.[2] Accordingly, EATWoT conferences were held in Accra (1977), Colombo, Sri Lanka (1979) and in São Paulo (1980). The fifth consultation in New Delhi (1981) once again assumed a fully intercontinental character. Its purpose was to evaluate the work done in the preceding years and to synthesize the theological project which EATWoT had launched. The common features and the differences between Third World Theologies were discussed, and also their relation to Western Theology. Under these conditions the time seemed ripe to convene a sixth EATWoT meeting in which representatives from the First World (Europe and America) were allowed to participate on an equal level.

However, only those men and women were invited who sympathized with the sociopolitical concerns of their Third World colleagues, and who themselves were busy developing analogous designs—e.g., Feminist Theology—and theological blueprints to justify and motivate the Peace and Ecology Movements. This historic global conference took place in January 1983 in Geneva, under the auspices of the World Council of Churches. The WCC demonstrated its sympathetic support by a pointed speech delivered by the hosting general secretary, Dr. Philip Potter.[3]

We shall return to the results of these EATWoT meetings later, but it is sufficient to say at this point that here a new kind and means of doing theology arose. This new theology's foundational principles have departed from all the traditional fundamental theological concepts. Such concepts were henceforth relativized and derogatively called "Western Theology."

2. "Christians for Socialism"

The second source of modern "People's Theology" is a movement called "Christians for Socialism" (CfS). It originated in 1968 in Chile and is most widely spread in Latin America. The first Latin American meeting of CfS took place in Santiago, Chile, from the 23rd to the 30th of April 1972. However, it was soon to cross international geographical boundaries. In 1975 an international conference of CfS was held in Quebec, Canada. From the beginning this movement was characterized by three distinguishing marks:

- The CfS proposed a "strategic alliance between revolutionary Christians and Marxists" to speed up the liberation of the Latin

American continent. Socialism is seen as the only valid alternative to the *status quo*.

- The CfS demanded that the Bible be read "in a new way." This came from the recognition that revolutionary praxis is the originating source for the new theological creativity.
- The CfS claimed that the gospel, read contextually in the light of the liberation struggle, leads to a deep criticism of the institutional church.[4]

The institutional church must be replaced, therefore, by an alternative church which emerges from the social basis and is intimately related to it. The name given to these basic ecclesiastical communities is "The New People's (or Popular) Church." In Spanish and Portuguese, the adjective *popular* carries a clear connotation of class struggle. The same applies equally to any similar term, especially the key concept "Theology of People" or "People's Theology."

3. Urban Rural Mission (URM)

The third source from which People's Theologies have originated is the theological work produced by the ecumenical movement called the Urban Rural Mission (URM). URM was formed in 1978 by the merger of two former subdivisions of the WCC, the Urban Industrial Mission (UIM) and the Rural Agricultural Mission. The URM coordinates teams of national and international workers who are involved in sociopolitical activities. Their leadership and inspiration comes from an international advisory group.[5] The URM's special concern is to fulfill the missionary mandate in a modern, contextual way by supporting the poor and powerless in their endeavors to change their living and working conditions. In order to conscientize the URM workers, the international advisory group holds consultations at strategic points in the Third World. These workers made a strong impact on the WCC conferences at Melbourne, Australia, in 1980 and Vancouver, British Columbia, Canada, in 1983.

The mission concept of the URM is oriented in a radical socio-ethical and political direction. Their aim is to help Christians in the

Third World understand that their "total mission" is the struggle for more justice.[6]

The URM's underlying theology is clearly expressed in a brochure that was published by the Christian Conference of Asia in 1977 under the title *Towards a Theology of People I*. In this brochure, the Church is represented as a people's movement whose members are recruited from the oppressed masses, following the alleged pattern of the Early Church in Palestine. Two years earlier at an UIM meeting in Tokyo, the international advisory group clearly opted for the ideology of class struggle.[7]

All URM groups try to arouse amongst the poorer church members a socio-revolutionary consciousness that is at the same time religiously motivated. The URM convenes theological consultations which are attended by theologians, church workers and influential laymen. Their purpose is to introduce conference attendees to the socio-critical method of reading the Bible. They teach that the texts of the Bible must be interpreted against the background of their own socioeconomic, political situation ("context"). The participants are charged to spread these ideas at the grass-roots level in their local churches.

In these conferences, the guiding thought is that the exploited people have the best understanding of the biblical texts because these texts were conceived in analogous situations. Theology, therefore, is primarily a concern of the People. The goal of such endeavors is to develop out of the "Responses of the People" a "Theology of the People." This idea of developing new theological perspectives from the spontaneously expressed opinions of simple Christians who speak from their own everyday experiences of oppression is also found, as we have seen, in the movement that we looked at previously, "Christians for Socialism" (CfS).

4. The Role of the World Council of Churches

Very early, the Ecumenical Center of the WCC exhibited its own keen interest in the development of such indigenous, contextual theologies, especially where these were characterized by an evident social and political dynamic. Thus in March 1973 a first symposium for representatives of North American Black Theology and Latin American Liberation Theology was held at the Ecumenical Institute at Bossey, near Geneva. It was here that the host Europeans were told in no uncertain terms that theological communication with them was impossible because there is no common ground between the oppressors and the oppressed! Two years later Dr. James Cone, the chief promoter of Black Theology, was invited to cooperate in the extended program of the WCC Assembly at Nairobi.

There is also clear evidence that the WCC is deeply interested in the socio-critical approach to the Bible as it is practiced in the Theology of the People. An early specimen is found in the October 1977 issue of the *International Review of Mission* (IRM).[8] Under the heading "Commentaries by the People," the results of an experimental project sponsored by Dr. Emilio Castro, then director of the WCC's Department on World Mission and Evangelism, are described. In this project he had asked a number of groups of laypeople spread over several continents to study two Lucan texts, the one on Jesus' sermon in Nazareth (Luke 4:16-30) and the other on Peter's fishing catch (Luke 5:1-11). He asked them to share their personal impressions against the background of their own life situation. From their remarks he hoped to receive answers to such theological questions as: Who is the subject of Christian mission? To whom is mission addressed? Who are our missionary associates? Which principalities and powers are encountered in mission today? What are their names? Here we have an early model of the procedure for building a "Theology of the People" as it is promoted by URM workers in several countries of the Third World.

Three years later, at the World Missionary Conference at Melbourne (1980), the same Bible study method was extensively used. The purpose of the Bible studies was to relate the second petition of the Lord's prayer, "Your kingdom come," to the various socioeconomic and political quests which were in the minds of the participants, especially those from the Third World.

PART II: THE METHODOLOGIES OF
THE "PEOPLE'S THEOLOGIANS"

The Dissociation from "Western Theology"

When the theologians from the Third World gathered together, their guiding motive, from the very beginning, was the quest for cultural autochthony. Their goal was to develop an indigenous theology which was to be a conscious antithesis of traditional theology, both with regard to its contents and its methodology. In the post-colonial era, the reaction to the Third-World nations which had also been felt in the urge of mission churches towards ecclesiastical independence now found its expression in a very emotional resentment in the realm of theology, which would sometimes lead to wholesale condemnations. "At present the theologies of Europe and North America are dominating in our churches," the participants of the first EATWoT conference stated in 1976. "They constitute a form of cultural domination."[9]

The Third-World theologians condemned Western Theology because of its academic form. They accused Western Theology of isolating thought from action. Therefore, they said, it is irrelevant to the vital issues of the Third World. They also felt that the traditional deductive method was too academic. This is the method by which theologians take Bible texts as the authority upon which to build theological reflection. In stating this, these theologians rejected, at least implicitly, the basic Reformation principle of *sola scriptura* — "Scripture alone." The Catholic principle of "Scripture and Tradition" did not fare any better. Instead, the Third-World theologians made a decisive choice for the "action-reflection model," under the influence of the Theology of Liberation. This is the model which is currently used in most departments of the World Council of Churches—except for the Faith and Order Commission.[10] According to this method, there is first of all a daring practical involvement. Only afterwards comes the rational, theoretical justification of the action. Concerning this, the theologians at the Dar es Salaam conference stated:

Regarding the epistemology, we are prepared for a radical break. We are ready to make engagement the first act of theology. We are ready to critically reflect upon the reality of the Third World as it represents itself in practice.[11]

The Choice for the Sociopolitical Struggle

The representatives of the new People's Theologies have rejected the deductive approach and replaced it with a pronounced alternative, the sociopolitical struggle. Thus we read in the resolution of the CfS Conference held in Quebec (1975):

> Many of us Christians have discovered the obligation to become practically involved in the liberating revolutionary struggle. It is in that struggle that we experience, reflect upon, participate in, and celebrate our faith in Christ. This has led us to recognize ever more clearly that the revolutionary task is the place where faith gains its true dimension and its radical, subversive power.[12]

From the other areas of the Third World comes an echo to this Latin American-inspired statement. The progressive Catholic Indian D. S. Amalorpavadas writes the following words, which "represent the views of many African and Asian Christians":

> The church has but one single mission, namely to be here and now the sign of Jesus Christ. She must make his liberating action present in the discouraging situation of our country by her engagement in the struggle of our people for liberation from the unjust and oppressive structures of our society. It is part of her witness that she identifies with the suffering masses, that she practises solidarity under the concrete conditions of the society in which she lives.[13]

According to this view, it is not even possible to distinguish between political involvement and theological work. Rather, the involvement in the liberation struggle of the People is the first step of action in this new type of theology. From this first step flows the fountain of understanding. It is from the understanding gained by participation in the liberation struggle that the content of the Church's teaching is to be derived.

The "People" as the Proper Subject of Theology

Who is the real subject in this action-reflection process found in the Theology of the People? Though it sounds unconventional, the answer is actually quite consistent. "The People" themselves are the subject(s) of theological reflection. "The People" themselves not only benefit from the results of this process, but are at the same time the agent of the theology which bears their name.

> The emphasis on *the people* as doers of theology is a recent development not only in the Philippines, but in many parts of the world.

So states Roman Catholic Sister Teresa Dagdag in her essay "Towards the Emergence of People's Theology in the Philippines."[14]

Because People's Theologians dissociate themselves from traditional Western Theology, they also are suspicious of any formation of a separate class of professional theologians. These professionals are so easily inclined to do their work in isolation from the larger community of ordinary Christians who should profit from their work. In contrast to this, the ordinary lay Christians are recognized as those who are able to do theology. This concept is taught without any reference to the traditional Reformation doctrine of the universal priesthood of all believers.

> It is the grassroots poor who are the authors and the producers of the theological formulations of which we are in search. They are the Theologians.[15]

It can, however, hardly be concealed that the grass-roots poor very seldom come to their theological insights by themselves. A considerable influence, although not always noted by the participants, is exercised by the animators of those contextual Bible discussions, which are often conducted according to group dynamics methods.

But who are the "People" to whom the simultaneous role of object and doer of theology is ascribed? The word *People* is not used in the same ethnological sense that was employed by a former German school of missiology. According to this school of thought, the establishment of an indigenous *Volkskirche* (People's Church), deeply rooted in the native social and cultural soil, was the aim of mission. Neither does the term *People* refer to the *laos tou Theou*— "people of God"—about which we read in 1 Pet 2:10. The "People," in other words, are not the Church of Jesus Christ as it is created by faith in the gospel and by baptism in the name of the Triune God. According to Leonardo Boff, the Latin American Spanish expression *popular* ("people") has a connotation different from the English usage. In the Spanish language *popular* is used, Boff states, to signify the working class, the poor, the oppressed, and the marginalized.[16] This means that the term *popular* or "people" is used with an emphasis on class struggle.

Thus, "the People" are the organized community of those who are materially poor, objectively oppressed, and aware of this oppression. They are the ones who fight against their oppressors in a radical, not just a reformistic, way.[17] The "Theology of the People" describes "the People" as the change-agents of history. It is "the People" who are elected to execute fully the process of liberation. This agrees perfectly with the theory of dialectical materialism.

Furthermore, in an ecclesiological perspective "the People"— the poor, not the hierarchy—form the primary subject of the Church. In the new "People's Church" ("the Church of the Poor") "the People" possess a prophetic and charismatic potentiality with which they are "endued" and are then "called" to question critically the validity of any ecclesiastical institution. The identity of the "people of God," then, is not constituted on dogmatic terms. *Rather, the identity is created in terms of solidarity with the social, political revolution.* Therefore, "the people of God" have principally an ecumenical, even an interreligious, character. *Since God sides with the poor, this People's Church is the only place where one can authentically meet God.* Therefore "the People" are the agent of evangelization—in the "holistic" sense, of course. In addition, they are, as we have pointed out earlier, the primary *doers* of theology.

The Steps in Developing a People's Theology

How do the People's Theologians concretely go about doing their work within the framework of this new model? What instructions are given to "the People" who are supposed to produce such theology? Since the whole movement is still in its experimental stage, no clear-cut, universally applicable manual can yet be expected, if ever. However, from my reading of their literature, I conclude that a number of practical steps seem to be taken in many cases. We shall try to analyze them as follows:[18]

(1) There must be a gathering of the representatives of "the People"—"the grassroots poor." The purpose of this gathering is to share with one another their recent experiences. There is usually a leader, sometimes a lay leader, and in certain cases also a theologian or priest. The leader stimulates and cautiously directs the group's conversation by asking provocative questions, mirroring their statements, or even giving suggestive interpretations.

(2) The participants are encouraged to reflect theologically on their contemporary life situation and history. This is done by relating to one another their personal experiences. The conversation is perhaps stimulated by a biblical text, a film, or a role play. Then attempts are made to interpret the contents.

(3) The participants' social, economic and political situation is now evaluated according to the methods of "scientific social analysis."

(4) This socially critical analysis is complemented by further consideration given in the light of the "biblico-historical faith." By this they mean that the Bible is to be treated as a textbook collection of liberation events in the history of Israel.

However, the Bible is not the only source of spiritual experience. Various proponents recommend at this step that the insights of native wisdom and native religion also be added. It is quite significant that non-Christian religions are regarded as part of the frame of reference for a People's Theology. This can be shown from the reports of many ecumenical consultations in the Third World. This is especially valid with respect to Asian—principally Indian—theologies (i.e., in contrast to a "contextually"-oriented direction in theology which is almost exclusively interested in the sociopolitical situation).

In the report of the EATWoT Conference in New Delhi 1981 we read:[19]

> People of other religions and creeds reveal some aspects of God's will and message for our time. Just as we Christians recognize the working of God in the events of Jewish history, so we also must learn to recognize the presence of God amongst the oppressed of other religions, who are fighting for their full humanity in the Third World today. Their sacred writings and traditions are also a source of revelation for us. If we consider this divine revelation, we are led to realize that the term "people of God" must be extended in order not only to include the believers of other religions, but the whole of humanity—all those on whom the God of the Bible wants to bestow life and self-realization.

No other statement could reveal the pan-religious, universalist character of the "Theology of the People" as clearly as this one!

(5) The results of the theological process are not confined to the formulation of new insights for interpreting the People's situation. If the work is done well, it must always lead towards new *action that brings structural change into society.*

A person demonstrates his understanding of "People's Theology" by participating in this society-changing action. Those taking part in these acts, however, include not only Christians, but *everyone* who belongs to the oppressed peoples. In common action with the adherents of other religions, further theological insights are discovered. *Dialogue*, then, with adherents of other religions and ideologies is not enough. At the EATWoT conference in New Delhi, it was stated:

> We support the ongoing dialogue between Christians and adher-ents of other religions. However, this dialogue cannot remain an intellectual discussion about God, redemption, human fulfillment or any other concept. In consequence of such dialogue there must be a joint involvement for a holistic liberation of the oppressed, not only an action that changes unjust and oppressive structures, but also attempts to regain our lost identity and our life giving values. Our joint action with people of other faiths is a valid source of theology in the Third World.[20]

Marxist Social Analysis

We referred to the "scientific analysis of the social situation" as the third step in the attempt to build a theology. By such "scientific analysis," the protagonists of a "Theology of the People" *always* have in mind a Marxist social analysis. This is openly advocated by the movement "Christians for Socialism," as well as by Latin American Liberation Theology. In addition, the consultations on People's Theology in Asian countries also acknowledge this Marxist social analysis. The Fifth Commission of the International Conference of "Christians for Socialism" in Quebec in 1975 declared:

> The attempt to differentiate between the options and founda-tional direction of the People's movement, has driven us to adopt a scientific Marxist analysis of reality, one which agrees with our class preference and serves as a support and a direction for action.[21]

In an essay about People's Theology in the Philippines, we read:

Perhaps one of the strongest influences or challenges to the Christian faith in the Philippines is MLMTT (Marxist-Leninist-Mao-Tse-Tung) ideology. To the question, "What is the Christian attitude to Maoist nationalism?" de la Torre says that: "Under concrete Philippine conditions, a Filipino Christian cannot make a Christian political choice if he does not seriously examine the challenge of Maoism. . . . For in the final analysis, to take the challenge of Maoism seriously is to take the Incarnation in Philippine society seriously; to analyse concrete situations and to side with the oppressed People in their struggle for liberation, not as a self-appointed leader but as a servant of the revolution. . . ."[22]

In addition, the first consultation of the Ecumenical Association of Third World Theologians in Dar es Salaam (1976) clearly expressed their sympathies with Socialism, though they tried to protect themselves by attempting to be critical of both sides. They pointed out the "notable results" of the socialist experiments in the People's Republic of China, North Korea, North Vietnam and Cuba. At the same time they gave recognition to the Soviet Union and Eastern Europe because they "often rendered assistance to the oppressed Peoples of other countries in their struggle for liberation." Even though some objected that Socialism has its own problems, especially the failure to uphold human freedom and the "price in human lives that the revolutionary process demands,"[23] this objection amounted only to a historical and philosophical apology for socialist oppression!

A final endorsement of this advocacy of a Marxist approach to social analysis comes from the WCC's headquarters itself. At the last EATWoT consultation in Geneva, in 1983, Philip Potter stated in his address to the delegates:

. . . it is significant to observe that we have been forced to the discovery of the realities of the Third World in their historic dimension, by the largely secular tools of analysis which have become available, especially Marxist analysis.[24]

The Socio-historical Hermeneutic

As we have seen in the description of the methodological steps by which a People's Theology is developed, the fourth stage provides that the present situation be perceived in the light of biblical history. We must come, then, to a very basic question—*the use of the Bible in the Theology of the People.* How much emphasis is laid on exegetical work, and what kind of hermeneutical principles are used?

When we compare the various models of socially and politically oriented Third World theologies, we can make a significant observation. Those in "Christians for Socialism" propose that the Bible should be read from a contextual, socio-historical point of view. This proposal has not only been accepted and methodologically refined by the Latin American Theology of Liberation, it has been integrated into practically all political theologies throughout the world. This is probably because this approach is recommended by WCC staff members and practiced at its meetings in their Bible studies.[25] It is assumed that the People's own historical experience of social misery conditions them to a sympathetic understanding of the biblical texts. The biblical texts are themselves understood as testimonies in which the ancient people of God enshrined their experiences of oppression and liberation. In this perspective the events are seen as a whole chain of redemptive events which point far beyond the era in which they were recorded. From this comes the conclusion that the whole history of mankind is one great process of God's liberating interventions.

Severino Croatto,[26] a leading representative of Liberation Theology, speaks about a "semantic axis" which is constituted by the constant sequence of promise and fulfillment, whereby each fulfillment of a past prophecy implies a new prophecy of even greater redemptive events in the future. This is especially deduced from Israel's experience in the Exodus from Egypt. The Exodus was viewed by the OT prophets as a paradigm within which to interpret God's saving acts in Israel's later history. In the NT, it is understood typologically to foreshadow the death and resurrection of Jesus Christ, who died and rose again for the sake of the redemption of all mankind from the bondage of sin. Liberation Theology, however, goes further and interprets this Christological Exodus as foreshadowing ever greater experiences of the corporate resurrections of whole nations in mankind's ongoing history. One recent example of this, to which reference is often made, is the "rebirth of the People of Nicaragua" through the Sandinista revolution. It is in this sense that Julia Esquivel, a lay leader from Guatemala, challenged the mission conference at Melbourne to show forth the faith of Abraham:

> . . . as it has been confessed again lately by the martyred Archbishop Romero of El Salvador. Predicting his own murder, he stated fearlessly: "If I am killed, I shall rise again in the Salvadorean People."

Continuing in this line, she states:

> Jesus, the Christ, preached and announced the Kingdom. He showed to us that the history of salvation is one with the history of the world of man. Israel is only one example. For us today Israel could be Zimbabwe, El Salvador, Nicaragua or Guatemala. . . . Each country has its own history of salvation. . . . Jesus is present and acts among the People as the Suffering Servant or as the Crucified King. . . . Jesus appears to us in the People, in their struggles, in their death, in their unity, in their hopes, and in the struggle for freedom.[27]

This is a striking example of the way in which the NT message is understood by "Christians for Socialism" and other representatives of the *popular* or "People's" Bible reading method. The biblical texts are used as symbols of political events that happen in contemporary revolutionary history.

The most radical use of socio-historical hermeneutics is made in the so-called "Materialistic Bible Reading,"[28] as it has been developed by several theologians in the Romanic countries of Western Europe, and which is continuously practiced by the CfS. According to this approach, it is assumed that Jesus should not be regarded as an individual person. As a result of the findings of historico-critical NT research, these theologians say, scholars can know very little concerning him. He should rather be viewed as the rallying point of a whole contemporary movement of marginalized and deprived people who might be called the "Jesus Movement." To them he proclaimed the Kingdom of God as an impending event in which all present sociopolitical conditions would be turned upside-down to the advantage of the poor.

A similar view is developed by the Korean scholar Ahn Byung Mu, one of the leading spokesmen for the Korean "Minjung Theology."[29] According to Ahn, the historic situation at the time of the NT was marked by the political tension between Jerusalem and Galilee. Jerusalem was the center of the oppressive rule, exercised jointly by the Roman occupants and the Jewish hierarchy. Galilee, on the other hand, became the refuge for the oppressed people, the *ochlos*. In addition the *zelotes* (Zealots), the freedom fighters of Israel, found their hiding-places and operational bases there. When Jesus, according to Mark 1:14f., decided to transfer his activities to Galilee, he thereby made a clear choice for the *ochlos* (for which the Korean equivalent is *Minjung*: "Minjung Theology," therefore, means "People's Theology"). They loved him and flocked around him, and he fully identified with them. Jesus, therefore, symbolized the aspirations of the poor and oppressed *Minjung*. As their representative, he was finally executed by the rulers in Jerusalem.

The Gospel of Mark most clearly upholds the Galilean base of Jesus, while Luke and John take a greater interest in his activities and destiny in Jerusalem. Ahn concludes, therefore, that this is a reflection of contending political options and theologies already in existence within NT Christianity. The present reader must choose between the various options in order to identify his own position with regard to today's sociopolitical struggle.

It should be quite evident that experimenting with such an unfounded hypothesis does not really contribute much towards a true understanding of the biblical message. It stands in open conflict with the way in which orthodox readers—and liberal ones as well!—have understood their Bible so far. As a matter of fact, the champions of "the Theologies of the People" are quite aware that they have to enter into completely new avenues in their "re-lectura"—that is, "rereading"—of the Bible. This, however, does not disturb them. They would answer this charge by claiming that the Bible almost always has been mishandled by priests and theologians throughout church history. Churchmen almost always have made the Bible's message serve the interests of the ruling classes. These priests have given an idealistic, otherworldly interpretation to the biblical texts so that their explosive contents would not disturb the consciences of the social oppressors and of the bourgeois Christians who sympathized with them.

The manifesto issued at a mass meeting of "Christians for Socialism" in Bologna states their case very bluntly:

> Today we can live in faithfulness to Christ and the poor only in the vitality of the revolutionary obligation. In doing so, we discover a totally new way of reading the Bible. . . . It is indeed an immense task. It is the rediscovery of the original meaning of the gospel and of its ability to do its work today. It is the task to which we feel obliged to jointly commit ourselves. It is the task which we regard as a reappropriation of the gospel by the poor, to which it rightly belongs and from whom it has been snatched away.[30]

The Chilean priest Estoban Torres places two foundational yet incompatible ways of reading the Bible next to one another. The one is the *bourgeois method* which, according to Torres, "is a godless, idol-serving, Bible reading method—a false search for God." The only legitimate Bible reading method, he says, comes from opting for the oppressed classes.[31]

According to the Portuguese theologian Fernando Belo, when someone "opts for the oppressed classes," he receives a new understanding of, for example, the whole Gospel of Mark as a "report concerning the practice of radical subversion." This subversive report in Mark's Gospel is supposed to have been covered up over the centuries by an idealistic, bourgeois exegesis which is opposed to a Materialistic Bible Reading method.[32]

The one who, with newly opened eyes, has so learned to read the Bible in this radically different manner does not need to remain with the canonical text. He will follow the suggestion of Dorothee Sölle and "write a new Bible," as the condensation of his experience of the movement of God in contemporary history.[33]

The Various Forms of "People's Theology"

If the primary subject of People's Theology is no longer that of an academically constructed theology, but "the People" in the sense of the poor and oppressed classes, this will have consequences regarding the form that this elementary theological activity takes. Yet the professional theologian is still judged to have a function in the process. He must give the necessary scientific form to the endeavors by writing theological monographs and by systematically designing, for example, a Theology of Liberation. However, it is "the People's" theological perceptions, in their own ways of expression, which are to be articulated in these new theologies. They can, for example, take the form of personal testimonies (Narrative Theology). They can take the form of new prayers, or poems, or songs. They can be whole liturgical forms, or even such nonverbal forms as cultic dances. The joy that many Third-World peoples find in drama can also be used to express certain theological perceptions by means of religious plays. An example of this was the play *Muntu* at the Fifth General Assembly of the World Council of Churches in Nairobi. Here an attempt was made to present the totality of African history. The person of Christ was "contextualized" in the play as a symbol of the timeless African corporate personality.[34]

This is one example of the attempts to meet the challenge given by Third-World theologians to use the witness of indigenous religions as a source of theological concepts. Another model example of these varying attempts is found in the booklet written by the Taiwanese theologian C. S. Song, entitled *The Tears of Lady Meng*. In this booklet, the author gives a symbolic meaning to an ancient Chinese mythological legend. In the legend, a widow gives her own

life as an offering for the salvation of her husband. Song uses this
to point in the direction of the hope that will be born out of the sufferings of the oppressed peoples of Asia.

Now it is clear that for these theologies the biblical material
is presented as only one element alongside of other equally acceptable elements. These other elements, of course, have their source in
non-Christian, indigenous mythology or even in the historical perspective of Dialectical Materialism. It is at precisely this point, then,
that the question of the Christian identity of such People's Theology
comes naturally and irrepressibly to the forefront. We shall return
to this crucial question in the conclusion.

PART III: THE CONTENTS OF PEOPLE'S THEOLOGY AND ITS ECUMENICAL SIGNIFICANCE

Earlier we saw that the advocates of a "Theology of the People" are
motivated by an emotional reaction against "Western Theology."
This reaction causes them to adopt a completely different *method*
of doing theology than that of traditional theology. This cannot fail
to produce serious consequences for the contents of such theology.
There is, of course, neither a unified system of People's Theology
nor a doctrinal textbook. In fact, both of these are excluded by
design. People's Theology wants "the People" at the grass-roots
level to express spontaneously their own theological persuasions.
These persuasions come as a response to the People's own social
experiences and their own encounters with biblical texts. At the
same time, we have very many recorded reflections on such a theology. Because of this, we can at least try to find out how the theologians of the People fill central theological themes with meaning.
That meaning is always relevant to the vital life situation of the
poor.

The Central Doctrinal Issues of People's Theology

Let me begin with the basic question which any theology—by
definition—must answer: *How are we to perceive God?*

God in the Movement of the People

We take it for granted that the cardinal concern of theology has always been the basic question about God himself. We are, then, astonished by the way in which this question is handled in the Theologies of the People. We find surprisingly few statements about God's person and nature. The point of departure when talking about God is a *negative* reaction to the way in which traditional Christian theology and piety have been speaking about God and to God up to now. This traditional theology is a real scandal to the advocates of People's Theology. They find this God associated with a social system which they profoundly abhor. They feel that traditional theology invokes God in order to legitimize such a system. They are revolted by the actual or supposed Quietism of Roman Catholic officials, or by the gospel proclamation of evangelical missions, or even by the corresponding piety of the masses. Concerning this, we can quote again from Julia Esquivel's wrathful cry of protest during the Melbourne conference:

> We had learned that God is a pure spirit; this affirmation in practice came to mean pure air, that is, empty words. . . . We have been discovering that in practice we have invented a God that sanctifies the system . . . that decides the price of oil or coffee or sugar; it is the same God who created and maintained that monster called the Shah of Iran . . . and Somoza in Nicaragua. . . . That God . . . disguises Himself with religious piety in order to defend us from atheism, or takes on the new attire of human rights. . . .[35]

Although Ahn Byung Mu from Korea discusses the experience of God in evangelical piety with less passion, he still writes with as negative a reaction as does Julia Esquivel. He refers to the strong trust in the power of prayer that is so typical of Korean church life. The relatives of prisoners had continued to pray to God, especially during the last decade of political pressure from the Korean military regime. They seemed attached to God like beggars, praying individually and together.

We are constantly hearing today about the miracles that are continuously occurring in the Pentecostal Churches. In these
churches there are mainly selfish prayer requests. Among us,
however, nothing of the sort has occurred—no such appearances
of God and no miracles. Among us, there is only violence and tor-
ture and, as a result, dying and injury. There is, therefore, the
reality of the absence of God. Is God dead for us? Is God only a
God for the rich, happy and smiling, and not for the suffering and
weeping?[36]

These shocking accusations remind us of the anti-religious
criticism of Karl Marx and his companions. They do not, however,
end up in atheistic cynicism. Rather, they lead towards a changed
understanding of God and our relation to him. God is no longer
thought of as a personal Being who is sovereignly enthroned above
the human world, yet near to all those who implore him in adora-
tion and petition him to intervene in their lives. Rather, he now
takes his place among the People themselves. He identifies with
them in such a way that he shares their suffering. At the same time,
he inspires them with new hope. This identification is so close that
it becomes impossible to distinguish between God's sufferings and
hopes and those of the People. The People, the Korean *Minjung*, or
the exploited Salvadorian urban and rural poor, become a new
incarnation of God. These theologians absolutely identify God in a
heretical, modalistic manner with Christ, the suffering Servant of
God. This is the God whom the People praise in the "People's Mass
of the Nicaraguans":

> You are the God of the poor,
> The human and humble God,
> The God that sweats in the streets,
> The God of the worn and leathery face.
> That is why I speak to you
> In the way my people speak
> Because you are God the worker,
> Christ the labourer.

This reminds us of the statement of such western socio-critical theologians as Dorothee Sölle. At first she became a theological atheist out of sympathy with the suffering—especially those gassed at Auschwitz. For these there was no God to come from the outside to avert their sufferings. Later, however, in a Hegelian sense, she placed God back into the historical process as an incomplete, suffering and hoping Being. Mrs. Sölle spoke in Vancouver (1983) of the "movement of God" in this exact sense. We take part in this movement through participation in the Liberation and Peace Movements.

Thus, according to People's Theology, God is present in the historical upheavals. He has become completely and totally one with the movement of the People. We cannot, therefore, avoid the question as to whether this God has not, in fact, become an abstraction. Has this God become a mere symbol or cipher of the corporate Self of the People who yearn and fight for their *own* deliverance?

To be sure, the working out of this salvation history is entrusted to mankind. It was in exactly this sense, when speaking about a "theology for the 1980's," that Dorothee Sölle claimed in Vancouver: "We have to democratize the idea of God." Doesn't this mean that the Lordship of the *Kyrios Theos* is replaced by the sovereignty of the People? Doesn't this mean that the two are now identified? *Vox populi, vox dei*—"The voice of the People is the voice of God."

The Diagnosis of Human Misery

Instead of making the doctrine of God our point of departure, we might certainly have been more sympathetic to the theologians of the People if we had started with their diagnosis of the human dilemma. All contextual theologies are conceived in an attempt to find a solution to the misery of the People today.

Unlike the book of Genesis, the representatives of a People's Theology do not see the root cause of human suffering in an apostasy from God in which each individual shares. For them, exploitation and oppression cause and determine the calamity to which the human masses in the Third World are exposed. This oppression causes their poverty. In the past the main culprit was western colonial imperialism. In the present the world's evils are produced mainly by neo-colonialism and by the worldwide economic system of capitalism. The military dictatorships of the Third-World nations, they teach, uphold and defend capitalism. The description and analysis of the evils inherent in the capitalist structures usually fill the first pages of the reports about consultations of Third-World theologians or whole chapters of textbooks on political theology.

The People's theologians always search for the guilty one *outside* the community with whose liberation they are concerned. The guilty one is mainly the political opponent, the agent of the economic system. Fault is also found with *Christian missions* because, it is alleged, they have collaborated in the colonial expansion. Fault is also found with *churches today* who silently condone this system and even benefit from it by their financial investments.

In contrast to such sharp accusations, a diagnosis of universal human sinfulness seldom occurs. This also applies to sin's expression in the evil actions of each individual, including the members of "the People." Raimond Fung's work is an example of this lack of diagnosis. He is a former Chinese UIM missionary and now is a staff member of the WCC's Department for World Mission and Evangelism. At the mission conference in Melbourne, he criticized evangelistic mission for addressing their listeners as sinners. Rather, the missionaries must realize that they are addressing the poor and the oppressed, who in actuality are the "victims of sin." These people are, in fact, themselves victims of other people's sins and should therefore be called "the sinned-against." This notion of "the sinned-against" was introduced at Melbourne as an important new category in theological language. Fung did not indeed wish to release totally the members of the People from their own sins. However, he did not see such sins in the light of a troubled relationship to God. *Instead, he saw them in terms of a lack of solidarity with the common liberation struggle.*[37]

Holistic Soteriology

The concept of salvation in the Theology of the People naturally corresponds with the given diagnosis of sin and evil. "Salvation" is the removal of the misery of the poor by the destruction of the socioeconomic and political power structures that are causing it. This holistic salvation is the envisaged goal of the fight for liberation, and in most cases the hope is to achieve it in the not-too-distant future. To quote again from Sister Teresa's lecture:

> Perhaps, for the first time in several centuries of Christianity in the Philippines, we Christians are beginning to take seriously the challenge of total salvation. The reality that the Christian needs to be liberated from all evil, physical, moral, psychological, political, economic, and social evils that dehumanize persons is very much felt in the Philippines. . . . The task is long and arduous, but it is one of the best moments of history because today, the new history is being written, the new society is being forged. . . .[38]

Salvation in People's Theology is essentially a dramatic term. It is accomplished by overcoming the evil, which, however, is not viewed in the form of real metaphysical enemies. The "principalities and powers" which must be overcome are the oppressive systems, *especially that of capitalism.*

What is missing in this concept is the biblical message about the death of Christ who as High Priest and Lamb of God gave his life as an expiatory sacrifice for our sin (cf. Hebrews 8—9). If this biblical thought is mentioned at all, it is either rejected or reinterpreted in such a way that it misses the mark. An illustration of this is the essay by Ahn Byung Mu about Minjung Theology:

> We had always been taught to understand the death of Jesus on the cross as an atonement. We always had the cultic sacrificial Lamb before our eyes. Thus we understood the crucifixion of Jesus only religiously and have interpreted the suffering of Jesus only as that of an individual. However, this was so very difficult for us to digest that we finally were compelled to overcome this strange thought pattern in order to understand. From our own

Sitz im Leben [context], the fact that the early church had already interpreted the passion of Jesus in the light of the Suffering Servant of God in Isaiah 53 received great significance. This suffering servant must not be understood as an individual but rather as a collective. May we from there not be allowed to see the cross of Jesus in direct relation with the suffering of the Minjung? What similarity is there between the behaviour of Jesus on the cross and the suffering Minjung? In the suffering Minjung we have met the suffering Christ. He was elected by the Minjung to be their scapegoat.[39]

It deserves to be mentioned that this interpretation of Isaiah 53 is not original to Minjung Theology. Its roots can be traced back to the rabbinical theologian Abraham Heschel. Pinchas Lapide also expressly applies it to the crucifixion of Christ. Jürgen Moltmann, who was in dialogue with Minjung Theologians, is likely to have picked up the interpretation and passed it on to Minjung Theology. Metropolitan Mar Osthathios, citing both Moltmann and Heschel, shared very similar thoughts in his message to the WCC's Melbourne conference entitled "The Gospel of the Kingdom of the Crucified and Resurrected Lord."[40] In spite of its alleged rediscovery, it is obvious that this interpretation of Isaiah 53 misses the decisive point. It teaches that the sacrifice was made for innocent, suppressed people, but Isa 53:5 shows that Christ died for *sinners*: "But he was wounded for our transgression, he was bruised for our iniquities; upon him was the chastisement that made us whole."

What, then, are the contemporary *means of salvation*? In order to answer this question, we have to consider the nature of the oppressive force which is to be overcome. At this point we find ourselves in a somewhat confusing situation because contradictory viewpoints are taken by the various representatives of political Third-World theologies. Most of the Latin American liberation theologians, especially those in "Christians for Socialism," would be inclined to advocate revolutionary violence. They justify this as self-defense and by the example of Jesus who cleansed the Temple by force. Theologians in the Far East such as Ahn Byung Mu of Korea and C. S. Song of Taiwan, on the other hand, have opted for a resistance without violence. They are convinced that there is an overcoming force inherent in the suffering of the powerless that will finally defeat the powerful oppressor. It was, for example, the tears of Lady Meng which pulled down the Chinese wall over the grave of her murdered husband. It was the silver fish, into which her smashed body changed upon its early death, which became the inextinguishable symbol of hope for which the People were longing. In this case, the parallel to Christ as Liberator is brought out through the fact that his vicarious death in solidarity with his people did not lead to the failure of his own hope. On the contrary, his death bestowed a new dynamic through the resurrection experience.

A comparative analysis of the two options will show that their apparent contradiction is not really rooted in principles of theological ethics. Rather, they are conditioned by the different situations. This conclusion is clear from the fact that all the representatives of political theologies sympathize with the armed struggle of the guerrillas in Latin American countries. In both cases the choice of means is legitimated by reference to the example of Jesus. The choice depends on the likelihood of successfully bringing about the desired goal, namely total liberation.

Jesus Christ

What we have observed concerning the treatment of the doctrine of God by People's theologians applies in the same way also to the doctrine of Jesus Christ. His nature and work are clearly not their primary concern. All, however, make reference to the historical Jesus as he has been newly rediscovered by the socio-critical Bible reading method. At the same time, this historical Jesus is not the starting point of our search for conscious direction for our lives based on his example and his proclamation. To find Jesus, one must go in the opposite direction.

We understand "to theologize" mainly to be the search for the contemporary Christ. Minjung Theology, therefore, is nothing other than the search for that contemporary Christ. Minjung

Theology has not first sought for Christ. It has first encountered the suffering Minjung and there has found an understanding of Christ's true face and his true reality.[41]

Jesus, then, is discovered in the faces and in the destiny of the suffering people, who are, in this case, the Korean *Minjung*. In the same way that God is largely identified with the People, Jesus is also most intimately associated with them. Ahn stresses that in his opinion it is not legitimate biblical exegesis to isolate Jesus from the *ochlos*, the People, who constantly surrounded him and with whose destiny he identified himself.

One must not look at the Minjung as the object [of mission] and Jesus as the subject. I have reflected upon the way of Jesus up to his cross in terms of this point of view. The crucifixion was not the crucifixion of the individual—Jesus—but the crucifixion of the suffering Minjung.[42]

Ahn's argument is similar to that of the proponents of the Materialistic Bible Reading method. He maintains that the fragments of the life history of Jesus had been presented in collective terms by the Early Church. When she represented Jesus in this way, she was not interested in his being in a metaphysical sense. She was interested in his relationship to people. The collective portrayal of Jesus by the Early Church is therefore important.

This collective or corporate Jesus is, however, not just an "event" of the biblical past. Today he becomes an "event" (i.e., not a person) in the present battles of the People. This is a concept which was also encountered in the "People's Mass of the Nicaraguans."

African Theology presents some direct parallels to both these examples from Asian and Latin American Theology. One example of this is in the play *Muntu*, which was performed at the WCC's Nairobi 1975 Conference. In this play Christ was torn out of his historical, biblical context. He thus could be used to represent those people who are alienated from their own culture and anthropologically impoverished. It was in this view of Christ as "representative man" that the African rediscovered his own authenticity. It is this same tendency which motivates representatives of black South African Liberation Theology to refer to Christ as being "black." By this they express their persuasion that Christ sides with the blacks in South Africa's racial conflict and that their suffering is his suffering. It is in this sense that some South African artists have depicted the crucified Christ as wearing the features of an African opposition leader such as Albert Lutuli or of a freedom fighter. This is a device which is also used by Latin American artists.

What is lost in this Christological view is the biblical "*pro nobis*"—"for our sake," in the sense that "Christ died for our sins." It was this biblical view which was so precious to Paul and to the Reformers. The above charge is not just an outsider's allegation. It is expressly maintained by Ahn Byung Mu himself: "I want to quite deliberately remove the idea that Jesus is there for the Minjung. He is *with* the Minjung."[43] Paul taught that the former is the prerequisite for the latter. That sense is lost here.

The Kingdom of God

Because People's Theology likes to express itself as a kind of Narrative Theology, it is far more interested in the Synoptic Gospels than in the reflective Pauline epistles or the meditative Johannine writings. The People's theologians focus the hope of the People on the proclamation of the Kingdom of God as found in the Synoptic Gospels. In the Theology of the People, the "Kingdom of God" embodies all their hopes for a future state of total salvation. This hope is often referred to by such words as "vision" or "utopia." It indicates that they have in mind a bright stage of history still far ahead and confidently trust in its coming. This confidence is quite evident in the way in which the hope for the Kingdom is unfolded. The participants of the EATWoT conference in Dar es Salaam characterized the contents of their hope, which they shared with all mankind, as "a new world order, which is founded on justice, brotherhood and freedom."[44]

The appeal given at that conference to all those who are doing theology in the churches implies that this goal is of an eschatological nature. The conference called on the churches "to join up with all those who are struggling to create a just world in order that all those who believe in Christ may actually participate in the struggle for a new world order and a new humanity." At the conclusion of their meeting, the participants pledged "to make the gospel relevant for all people and, as God's fellow-workers, to cooperate joyfully in fulfilling the divine plan of salvation for the world."[45]

This vision of the future, although passionately upheld, seldom stretches beyond the history of this *present* world. Even when the biblical promise of the eschatological Kingdom is quoted literally, it is closely associated with the historic hope for this present world. Sister Teresa Dagdag makes this quite evident when she concludes her lecture on the Philippine Theology of the People with this pathetic exclamation:

> It is one of the best moments of history because today, the new history is being forged. The Kingdom of God, His reign of justice, is being established in this country of 7000 islands.[46]

If confronted, many People's theologians would deny that they expect the complete fulfillment of the biblical promises of the Kingdom within time and history. These promises, they would say, will completely appear only outside of time, in the Eschaton. However, nowhere does this concept find a central position in their theology.

PART IV: A CRITICAL EVALUATION OF THE THEOLOGY OF THE PEOPLE

At the conclusion of this analysis of the various ecumenical Theologies of the People, we cannot avoid stating our own judgment of it. In doing this, we are perfectly aware of the fact that its representatives reject the ability of western theologians to render a fair criticism. The reason for this, they claim, is that People's Theology is born out of an experiential involvement, something which westerners do not have. In answer to this, we might note that theology knows of no cultural separation. "Theology" means to reflect on the essence of the Christian faith in the light of God's biblical revelation. It is a responsibility which is laid upon the entire Church of Christ and which is performed in mutual service by her members for each other.

Legitimate Concerns

First, we recognize that the representatives of the various proposals for People's Theologies are moved by the very real needs of their nations, especially their lower classes. They have been observant and have shared in their sufferings with sympathetic hearts, as is expected from any true follower of Jesus. Many of them have taken sacrificial risks in their involvement. We know of UIM workers such as the Indian Harry Daniel whose involvement in the Philippines ended in a painful arrest.

The description of the social needs of the poor which these theologians give in the analytical parts of their presentations are impressive and realistic. They cannot be lightly dismissed, even if one does not share their so-called "scientific social analysis," which is usually determined by Lenin's theory that imperialism is the final attempt to prevent the collapse of capitalism.

We recognize the urgent concern to establish the social-ethical implication of the Christian faith as an important theological task, although we cannot follow their lead when theology and social ethics are equated *in toto*.

We also concur with the claim that theology must aim at the upbuilding of the entire Church and that the theological statements must be translatable into the practical, everyday experience of ordinary believers, including the poor in their various social situations. The Christians of Asia, Africa, Oceania and Latin America are entitled to receive an authentic answer to their questions. Why is there so much suffering? What really is the foundation of their faith? What is the goal of their hope? These deep human concerns should not be handled by theological educators in the Third World in an abstract, merely doctrinal way. They must always be dealt with in concrete relation to the circumstances under which such questions arise. No missionary will deny that the task of inculturating the gospel has only been partially solved by Christian missions and national churches—if at all.

Finally, we admit that the Bible has much more to say than what individual Christians or even entire confessional traditions have found in it and internalized into their own belief systems. We all have our blind spots. It is quite possible that if we approach Scripture from a new perspective and with new questions, we could discover surprisingly new aspects of the divine Word—very likely also with regard to our socio-ethical values and behavior. No exegetical school has exhausted the whole biblical truth. Thus, I am quite open to enter into dialogue with the representatives of a socio-historical approach to the Bible in order to gain new insights, provided they are not so ideologically biased that the plain message is obscured from the start.

Ideological Distortion of the Biblical Faith

This last-mentioned reservation embodies my decisive complaint against these new People's Theologies as we have come to know them. The price which is paid in the endeavor to attain a new theological relevance with regard to the vital needs of the Third World's poor is frightening and can hardly be justified from a Christian position which tries to cling to the faith once for all delivered to the saints. In our presentation of the methods and contents of the ecumenical Theologies of the People, we have shown that these new theologies constitute a *consistent and radical alternative* to the historic faith of the Church. This radical alternative to historic Christianity is not only admitted to but also openly propagated by its advocates, though they cannot demonstrate that it is authentically Christian by supplying objective theological criteria. The Christian faith and theology are subjected to an action-oriented utilitarianism. They can legitimate this new theology from the Bible only if they either eliminate important opposing biblical statements or hazardously reinterpret them. How can one possibly state that it is the task of Christian theology "to joyfully cooperate in fulfilling

God's plan of salvation for the world" (implying that this plan aims at the establishment of a new world order and the creation of a new mankind) if one relegates God's majestic promise "Behold I make all things new" (Rev 21:4) to the realm of mythology?

We have seen that all the proponents of the various People's Theologies, regardless of their regional distinctions, maintain that Marxist social analysis is a legitimate and indispensable tool. It is not only valuable for social analysis but also necessary for the development of a truly contextual, relevant Christian theology. The gospel is chained, thereby, to an ideology which from its very inception has been its decided opponent. Not only this, but *the gospel and Marxist analysis are totally irreconcilable in their foundational principles*. The result is, as we have seen in the selected examples of their doctrinal statements, a consistent estrangement from the biblical message. All scriptural terms are filled with a new, often opposite meaning. The result is a radical change in spiritual substance. What Bishop Bonaventura Kloppenburg has stated with reference to "Christians for Socialism" holds true also with respect to the development of other sociopolitically oriented People's Theologies:

> According to all the proponents of this new People's church, the Faith as it has been delivered to us is seen merely to be an ideologized, domesticated, and distorted faith. Therefore these people urgently demand—the following expressions are their own—a "de-ideologization of the faith," "a new interpretation of the faith," "a transformation of the faith," "a new formulation of the faith," "a purification of the faith," "a re-reading (re-lectura) of the faith," "a new design for the faith," "a new expression of the faith." The Christian conscience of the "Christians for Socialism" regards political emancipation as a challenge. It is a challenge which brings into question the entire dogmatic system of the institutional church.[47]

The Surrender of Biblical Soteriology

The People's Theologies are introduced as relevant interpretations of that salvation which is proclaimed in the Bible and achieved by

Jesus. In reality, however, as we have seen, the biblical concept of salvation is so completely altered that any connection between the scriptural statements and the postulated sociopolitical realization of this salvation cannot be proved by any firm exegetical or dogmatic standards. The person of Jesus Christ is submerged in the anonymous collective of the masses struggling for political liberation. Because of this, his atoning act, as it is related and interpreted in the NT Gospels and epistles, can no longer be recognized. That central atoning act must give way to those types of liberating changes which modern people in their different situations are longing for and are urgently demanding.

The result is a total leveling of the vertical relation between God and man into a purely horizontal, social dimension. People's Theology finds no place for the restoration of the disrupted relationship with God. This relation, distorted by sin at the Fall, is the overcoming of the human predicament at its deepest level. This applies also to the misery of the Third-World poor, if we take into consideration that they themselves are sinners and "sinned-against" at one and the same time. Indeed, they are sinners as well as victims of the sins of other fallen human beings who need reconciliation. The present and eschatological hope of victory over all suffering is a consequence of the basic work of Christ's salvation.

The Danger of Man's Self-Deification

Even more fatal than this distortion of the biblical salvation is the loss of a personal dimension in the concept of God in Jesus Christ. We have seen that the proponents of People's Theology are so ensnared by the analysis of corporate human suffering that the quest for God or the answer to his calling hardly ever come within the purview of such theology. Both appear merely as a symbolic mirroring of one's own corporate suffering, hope or liberating experience. The result is that the names "God" and "Jesus Christ" actually serve as virtual code symbols for the People themselves. As any rate, it becomes virtually impossible to distinguish between the two; i.e., the People, in effect, become "god." This observation is emphasized by the strong measure of responsibility that such theology ascribes to the People in the realization of their own liberation. They equate this liberation, in turn, with the carrying out of the divine plan of salvation.

In this process, the danger is that theology will lose sight of its central subject. When, however, the People's theologians use the name "God" to denote humanity's own destiny, they ascribe to man in his corporate appearance divine dignity and power. Moreover, they are preparing to let collective humanity take the place of God and his Son (cf. Psalm 2). With this, the primal temptation of the snake in the Garden gains a frightening new relevance and actuality: "*Eritis sicut Deus!*" ("You shall become as God!"—Gen. 3:5).

Are Third-World People's Theologies Universal or Indigenous?

Trutz Rendtorff[48] warned us that the inherent universality of theology is endangered by the outbreak of independent theologies in the Third World. This could make impossible a necessary theological communication. We have already mentioned that James Cone at the first Consultation of the proponents of Black Theology and Liberation Theology in 1973 rejected out of hand any possibility of such theological communication between the "advocates of the oppressors and the oppressed."

It is the proud boast of the proponents of those movements developing the various Theologies of the People that for the first time in history the Christians of Asia, Africa and Latin America are formulating their own expressions of faith in a way truly contextual to their own situation. At the end of our survey we have, nevertheless, to ask the question: "How objectively true is this claim, and how spontaneously independent from western patterns and influences are these theological formulations?"

This last question imposes itself upon us simply because it appears very difficult to explain the obvious similarity between all these theological drafts which have appeared almost simultaneously in different continents and countries apart from common sources.

The participants of the EATWoT Conference in their first report (1976) answer this question by referring to the common experience of people of the Third World who became victims of past and present imperial expansion of the West. However, it makes one wonder why such analogous new theological patterns did not appear earlier, especially since there were various attempts to develop indigenous theologies, especially in Asia. Indeed, it is strange that now, almost simultaneously, in every area of the world Marxism should appear as a decisive aid for providing relevant answers to the needs of the Third World, especially since there is a tremendous sacrifice of biblical content when Marxist concepts are accepted.

We can trace the history of the report produced by the EATWoT New Delhi 1981 Conference, entitled *Irruption of the Third World—A Challenge to Christian Theology*.[49] When we do so, we discover that from the outset there has been a communication of Western Theology to the representatives of the Third World. During recent years the Ecumenical Movement has systematically coordinated all attempts to develop such "Theologies of the People." We may observe certain distinctions in the local coloring and in the terminology in the various geographical regions, but the basic tenets and objectives have been similar or even identical.

We have already pointed out the mediating role which was played by the WCC through its international advisory group, the URM, in opting for the class struggle model in every situation in which their coworkers were engaged. In the report of the first meeting of EATWoT, we read that this new association was financially supported by two circles in North America and Europe. We also know their members as well-known protagonists of revolutionary political theology—George Casalis, François Houtard, Paulo Freire, Julio de Santa Ana, and Johann Baptista Metz.[50]

In both style and contents, the Dar es Salaam report clearly reveals the hand of the convening secretary of this consultation, Sergio Torres. He is well-known as a radical proponent of the Latin American Theology of Liberation. Such identification easily solves the riddle of how a meeting, composed of participants from such different backgrounds, could reach such a measure of consensus in just a few days.

We can go further and point out that the Latin American Theology of Liberation itself is not a plant indigenous to that continent. Its leading representatives studied in Europe and worked in close interaction with European theologians. The decisive impulse to create such a theology was given during the lecture tours through Latin American countries of two vocal proponents of political theology in Germany—viz., Jürgen Moltmann and Johann Baptista Metz. Those in "Christians for Socialism" in Latin America are also deeply indebted to European thought. The Materialistic Bible Reading method is their most important theological tool, by means of which they try to give a biblical motivation to their revolutionary engagement. That in itself was invented by Roman Catholic theologians in Spain, Italy and France. In a similar manner, we can trace the origins of the South African Black Liberation Theology to its proponents' personal contacts with representatives of Black Theology in the United States.

The circle closes with the events of the sixth EATWoT conference in January 1983 in Geneva. There only 40 percent of the participants came from Third-World countries, while the remaining 60 percent was made up of proponents of western theologies which, in their basic thrust, stand in perfect agreement with the political theology of the Third World. In Geneva 1983, the real provocation was not stirred up by the peculiar ideas of Third-World theologians who insisted on their own cultural identity. It came, rather, from the extremely pointed propositions found in the speeches of the western lecturers—viz., J. B. Metz, D. Sölle, G. Casalis and Rosemary Ruether.

This meeting took place in the headquarters of the WCC. The general secretary of the WCC expressed to the delegates his sympathy with this type of socio-critical theology in the Third World. These facts, then, are a final confirmation of my thesis that the so-called Theologies of the People owe their emergence largely to ecumenical initiative, funding and coordination.

Earlier we asked how indigenous and how universal the

Theologies of the People in the Third World really are. Our conclusion must surely have been disquieting. This leads us, then, to
several very important questions:

(1) Does the theological problem of the Ecumenical
Movement really lie in the difficulty of mediating theologically
between the historic, western tradition of the Christian faith and the
attempts of the younger churches in the South and in the East to
express the same Judeo-Christian faith in their own culturally conditioned categories, with relevance to their social needs?

(2) What is the real problem of the Ecumenical Movement
when it strives to secure understanding, cooperation and spiritual
unity thus between the older and younger churches?

(3) Does the basic problem not rather consist in the fact that
the World Council of Churches has introduced a new ideologically
inspired view of universal salvation?

(4) Have they not introduced this by systematic indoctrination
and coordination both to the younger and the older churches?

(5) Doesn't this stand in conflict with the faith held by them
thus far?

(6) Does this not confront Christians everywhere with a
choice—either to hope for a transcendental perfection of their salvation in the City of God which comes down from heaven, or to
accept an inner-worldly eschatology in the City of Man built by
himself?

Obviously the latter is an alternative to the traditional
Christian faith which might well prove to be far more radical
than any previous deviation with which the Church's teaching
ministry has had to cope thus far. The fascination of its proposals not only captures the minds of the lesser educated, but also
confuses the spiritual discernment of many high-ranking church
leaders and theologians both in the East and in the West. We can
see this, for example, in the present battle that is raging within
the Roman Catholic Church concerning the validity of
Liberation Theology.

(7) Does this not then threaten us with a new cleavage of
Christendom which, on account of the radical change in the historic

biblical faith, will add immeasurably to our historic confessional separations?

To some readers these questions may appear a little too dramatic and exaggerated. However, in the light of the material presented to you, it appears to me that the issue is serious enough to merit—indeed require—careful investigation.

WHAT KINGDOM IS AT HAND?
A Critical Assessment of
The Kairos Document

INTRODUCTION

In the previous chapter I sought to examine the sources, methodologies and contents of what has come to be known as "People's Theology." In dealing with the question of methodology, I outlined four practical steps which appear to be taken by most "People's theologians" as they seek to construct such a theology. In fact, this was precisely the procedure adopted by the so-called "Kairos Theologians" who produced *The Kairos Document*, to which we must now give attention.

On the 25th of September 1985, Dr. Beyers Naudè, general secretary of the South African Council of Churches (SACC), introduced to the leaders of the WCC's Ecumenical Center in Geneva a theological statement which, as its heading stated, was meant as a "Challenge to the Church." It was addressed not to any particular church, nor to the members of the SACC alone, but to the entire Christian community in the world.

The name given to the publication is *The Kairos Document*,[1] and its character is described in the preface as "a Christian, biblical and theological comment on the political crisis in South Africa today." The Geneva staff accepted this challenge immediately since the South African conflict has always ranked very high on the WCC's agenda, especially after the launching of its Programme to Combat Racism (PCR) in 1969. Soon *The Kairos Document* (KD) was translated into several languages and was sent to the main member churches of the WCC with a request to comment on it. In Germany, for example, the distribution was handled by the Evangelisches Missionswerk (Hamburg), which sent the KD to all delegates of the National Synod of the Evangelical Church in Germany (EKD) and also provided a detailed comment by its Theological Commission.

The indications are that the KD is being regarded as of utmost theoretical and practical significance both in the theological and the political realm, not only by its sponsors, but also within all major sections of the Ecumenical Movement. For the African Christians in South Africa, it is rapidly becoming a symbol and embodiment of their religiously sanctified claims for liberty and restitution.

In contrast to this, the origin of the KD is still rather obscure. Although the list of its original signatories contains about 150 names of ministers and lay members of all major denominations in South Africa, including the Roman Catholic Church, the real author (or authors) has chosen to remain anonymous. This is a poor reflection upon its confessional stance.

It is known, however, that the KD has a definite relationship to the Institute of Contextual Theology in Johannesburg and that it is the product of three meetings in Soweto. A careful study of a contemporary lecture,[2] delivered before the West German Rhenish Synod by Dr. Wolfram Kistner, the theological secretary of the SACC, will show that the KD has been influenced very strongly by his personal theological and political views. A similar influence has been exerted by Dr. Beyers Naudè, who has championed the cause of the KD in the Ecumenical Movement.

The KD is not, as a close analysis can show, an autonomous product of the South African soil in the present national situation.

Rather, it is a locally colored specimen of a modern thrust of ecumenical theol-political thinking which is classified aptly by the term "contextual theology." Without a close interaction between the author(s) of the KD and other representatives of this theological movement, the document could not have been written.

The KD of 1985 was only the first of several other *Kairos* documents which followed its pathway since then. In July 1987, on the initiative of the Reverend Cesar Molebatsi (Soweto), one of the original signers of the KD, a very similar document was published under the title *Evangelical Witness in South Africa*.[3] It uses a more evangelical terminology, but follows a similar line of thought and uses the methods of contextual theology. In April 1988 a group of theologians from Nicaragua, Costa Rica, El Salvador, Mexico, Panama and Guatemala published a declaration called *The Central American Kairos. A Challenge to the Churches and to the World*.[4] On July 31, 1989, in a press conference in London, Dr. Allan Boesak and other South African churchmen presented to the public an international *Kairos* document called *The Road to Damascus*.[5] This document was also published in South Africa, Namibia, South Korea, the Philippines, El Salvador, Nicaragua and Guatemala. As stated in London, the document was the outcome of a two-year process of consultations between theologians of these seven countries on the initiative of the South African Institute of Contextual Theology. The main sponsors in South Africa were the Rev. Dr. Allan Boesak, president of the Reformed World Federation, Archbishop Harry Ngada, Archbishop Desmond Tutu, Dr. Wolfram Kistner and Father Smangaliso Mkatshwa, general secretary of the Institute of Contextual Theology. This clearly shows that *Kairos* theology has developed into a worldwide ecumenical movement during a very few years! Both with regard to the basic dogmatic persuasions and to methodology, all the documents reveal the same origin. We, therefore, can confine ourselves to analyze the original *Kairos Document* of 1985.

The KD is clearly divided into five chapters with a short conclusion which advises its readers regarding its use and its practical implementation. Its contents can be summarized as follows: The first chapter translates the Greek name *kairos* with the heading "A Moment of Truth." It stresses the then present phase in the history of South Africa's political conflict—the upheaval of the year 1985—and identifies it as a divinely appointed time of utmost significance both for conscientization and action for all Christians inside and outside South Africa.

The second and third chapters engage in a severe criticism of the thinking of the authors' political and ecclesiastical opponents, thus preparing by a *via negativa* the introduction of their own revolutionary concept of a contextual theology which responds creatively to the challenge of the South African *kairos*, both in word and action.

The opponents of the sponsors of the KD are divided by them into two groups. The first consists of all nominal Christians who, either in politics or in church life, uphold the present political system of a segregated state and society ruled by a possessing white class. Their attempts theoretically to legitimize the *status quo* by biblical, ideological and political arguments are named "State Theology." This theology is not only criticized, but condemned in the harshest language.

The other group is seen to stand not in a hostile but rather a neutral attitude to the sponsors. It consists of those churchmen, mostly leaders and laypeople in the white, English-speaking denominations, who basically are in favor of sociopolitical change in South Africa. Such people want to see those changes brought about by nonviolent, evolutionary means rather than by a revolutionary way and seek to justify their stance by conservative, biblical arguments. Their thinking is labeled as "Church Theology" and is criticized by a theoretical attack on its three cardinal concepts—viz., "Reconciliation," "Justice" and "Non-violence." Added to this criticism is a diagnosis of this group's "Fundamental Problem," which consists in its proponents' adherence to an allegedly outdated, traditional approach to theology which lacks the empirical dimension of social analysis and political strategy.

In contrast to this, the fourth and fifth chapters outline the sponsors' own concept of "doing theology" in a revolutionary situation. They call this new pattern a "Prophetic Theology" which radically exposes and opposes the socioeconomic evils of the prevailing political system of oppression and voices a message of hope for immediate and radical change. This "Prophetic Theology," therefore, leads in the fifth chapter to a "Challenge to Action." Assuming as a theological undergirding that "God sides with the oppressed," it consists of detailed counsel to the churches and their members regarding participation in the present revolutionary struggle. This involves the transformation of all traditional church activities including divine worship, the administration of the sacraments, and pastoral counseling so that they conform to and inspire this political involvement.

In the "Conclusion" the sponsors address themselves to the Christians in South Africa and encourage them to meet everywhere in small circles in order to develop these themes. This is promoted and coordinated by an organizational office which employs several full-time staff members. "There is nothing final in this document," the authors assure their readers in spite of their claim that "this challenge comes from God." It is on this basis that they engage in action.

Fellow Christians throughout the world are entreated to give their necessary support to this cause so that the South African bloody struggle may be brought to a speedy end—in line with the sponsors' own political goals, of course!

THE KAIROS DOCUMENT AS A PARTICULAR SPECIMEN OF CONTEXTUAL THEOLOGY

The KD must be seen within the wider framework of the contemporary ecumenical thrust for a new way of doing theology relevant to those social, economic, cultural and political changes which may appear desirable or even necessary in the eyes of their proponents. During the last twenty-five years, a whole tradition of such down-to-earth types of theology has emerged and been developed, all more or less related to each other, while each one is molded in such a way that it fits the particular regional or functional interest in mind. Such theologies would include: "The Theology of Secularization" which has its roots in the writings of Friedrich Gogarten and Dietrich Bonhoeffer; "The Theology of Hope" which took its rise in the neo-Marxist thinking of Ernst Bloch and the Frankfurt School under its name "Critical Theory" (Marcuse, Habermass, Adorno); "The Theology of Revolution," which, in different shades, was called for at the Geneva Conference on Church and Society in 1966; "The Theology of Liberation," a refined version of the Theology of Revolution, which originated (under European inspiration) in Latin America at about the same time as its North American counterpart; "Black Theology" (James Cone). The Latin American Theology of Liberation and the North American Black Theology were soon being exported to other continents, giving rise to regional and cultural adaptations. These, as we have seen,[6] would include the "Homeland Theology" of Taiwan, the "People's Theology" of the Philippines, and "Minjung Theology" in South Korea. At the WCC's World Missionary Conference at Melbourne in 1980, the "Theology of the Poor" was introduced to the Ecumenical Missionary Movement as a guideline for a missionary strategy which focuses on the liberation of the poor as the main intention of Christ's proclamation of the Kingdom of God.

When in December 1976 in Dar es Salaam the Ecumenical Association of Third World Theologians was established, all these different versions (plus several types of indigenous theology that put a high value on inculturation) were brought into an even closer contact and interaction under the umbrella of "Contextual Theology." It is of interest to note that from the very beginning this movement for Third-World theology also included representatives of western emancipatory political theology, and that "Feminist Theology," represented by outspoken women such as Rosemary Ruether and Dorothee Sölle, was also soon admitted. This soon began to play an important role in paving the way towards a new, relevant theology of the eighties.

Two observations may be added here:

First, the champions of such theology are persuaded that it is eventually bound to replace the traditional form of theology both with respect to its methodology as well as its content, since only in this way can the challenge of the new age be met.

The second observation is that from the very beginning the WCC has taken a keen interest in such theology and has served as its seedbed, promoter and coordinator. The general secretary of the SACC knew very well that his KD would receive a very sympathetic and cooperative audience when he chose the WCC's headquarters as the platform from which to introduce the document to the public. It is more than probable that the WCC and some of its accredited theologians had been involved in the conceptional stage. The whole pattern and language of the KD sound very familiar to the ears of those acquainted with conciliar theology in recent years.

Basic Features of Contextual Theology

We should observe some of the basic features of such ecumenically accredited "contextual theology" and may note the following points:

(1) Contextual Theology (CT) begins with a deliberate break with traditional theology as it has been developed and practiced within the Christian Church in all its confessional branches throughout its history. Traditional theology has been discarded because, in the opinion of the proponents of CT, (a) it is too abstract; (b) it is irrelevant to the real problems of our present epoch of history, problems which are basically concerned with the social human development; and (c) it has always been inclined to justify and to give sanction to the political *status quo*. This makes it a kind of court theology siding with the established rulers against the vital concerns of the lower classes of society.

(2) The distinguishing methodological mark of CT is that it replaces the deductive by an inductive method. While in classical theology the authority of a given text in the Bible or the Church's creed is the starting point, contextual theology starts with the present social situation of the reader and makes his social quest the supreme motive and even a canonical rule for finding relevant the-

ological answers. The method by which this situation or context is to be interpreted is the so-called *social analysis*. It is a basic step towards attaining any theological knowledge and precedes even the reading of the Bible. Typically, the KD identifies the fundamental problem of "Church Theology" as its failure to specify and employ "social analysis" as a most important task of theology.

(3) The social analysis employed by the proponents of such contextually relevant theology is invariably borrowed from the Marxist social philosophy according to which the underlying principle of the dialectical process of history is the class struggle between the rich and the poor, between the oppressor and the oppressed. This point of view pervades the entire KD and provides its inner dynamic and consistency.

(4) Only after having made an assessment of the present historical situation by means of "social analysis" does contextual theology turn to the Bible. However, it uses it in a critical manner. Most representatives of contextual theology trace the alleged ideological tendency of traditional theology back to the authors of the books of the OT and NT. Here the former literary criticism of modern exegetical research is replaced or supplemented by the social critical approach. In its most radical form, especially as it is practiced in the movement "Christians for Socialism," this hermeneutical approach is called "Materialistic Bible Reading" or "*Materialistic Exegesis*."[7] The basic question is not, for example, "What does the Holy Spirit say to us through this Word of God as related by the evangelist Luke?" but rather, "Of whose social interests does this given text or textual tradition take care?" This means that the Bible is read and interpreted under a selective principle; thus, texts which do not support the social interest of the reader have their abiding significance reduced by being treated as if they were of situational importance alone. Alternatively, they are reinterpreted contrary to the author's original intention. Failing this, the texts are evaded or discarded altogether.

The KD's selective use of the Bible leaves out broad strands of teaching altogether while some texts—for example, Romans 13— have their binding authority toned down. Others—for example, the

sermon of Jesus in the synagogue of Nazareth (Luke 4:18-19)—
are forced to support the biased views of the proponents of social
analysis. This points clearly in the direction of a socio-critical
hermeneutic.

(5) In the ecumenical movement for contextual theology, the
underlying concern is not the attaining of divine *knowledge* leading to a deeper understanding of God's mind and to closer fellowship with him. It is, rather, the motivation for *action*, action in the
sociopolitical, economic sphere. Since the context in which such
theology is practiced is always considered as a state of misery, the
action aimed at by such theology is an involvement in the political
struggle.

(6) In the dialectical movement between theoretical understanding and practical action, the latter always has priority. The
people who are resorting to contextual theology are already
involved in a political struggle. They have already taken some
action to change their situation. Theology, for them, has the function of giving a deeper explanation of the rationale of such action
and in this way imparts to it a kind of divine sanction.

In the WCC, which in recent years has more and more followed this approach, this theological method is called the "action-
reflection model." Here the action precedes the reflection. The
function of the reflection is to understand our involvement in the
historical process and why we have been led, together with our non-
Christian fellow participants, to act in the way in which we did.
This means that the action which fits the situation sets the norm,
not a given biblical text which is introduced into the situation from
outside.

The legitimation for this pragmatic principle, which would
have offended our theological forebears, is attempted by advancing
the idea that God himself is seen as being involved in history.
Indeed, God is to be seen mainly or only in the midst of the historical process for the liberation of humanity, with whose destiny,
struggle and hope he is totally identified. It is in the crucial moments
of history, where decisive action becomes possible and indeed

imperative, where this God of human history reveals himself in his purpose to bring about his Kingdom.

THE IDENTIFICATION OF THE REVOLUTIONARY SITUATION WITH THE DIVINE *KAIROS*

The very name which the sponsors have given to their declaration, *The Kairos Document*, shows that they regarded the present moment within the history of South Africa, its people and its churches as crucial. The world *kairos*, as it is used here, implies two central elements. One is the urgency of the present political situation as a time to make decisions and to act. The additional element is that this historic moment is given a biblical or prophetic interpretation. It is the moment of truth, "the moment of grace and opportunity, the favourable time in which God issues a challenge to decisive action."[8] It is also the day of judgment on the Church in South Africa, a time which must not, under any circumstances, be simply allowed to pass by.

The attempt to claim for the present moment in history the dignity of a divine *kairos* is not new in modern religious history. At the beginning of this century, the religious socialists also spoke of the present moment as a *kairos* which the Church had to seize under all circumstances to fulfill her social mission. Later on, the very worst example was given by the church party of the German Christians. They believed that the coming of Adolf Hitler to power made the year 1933 one of the great moments of history when God himself had intervened. This brought kairological thinking into disfavor, at least in continental theological circles. However, within the Ecumenical Movement it has again become fashionable to look at secular history as the particular realm in which God is at work in revelation, in judgment, and in grace. This perspective has been introduced into the conciliar movement, especially by the Indian lay theologian M. M. Thomas, who served as the WCC's Central Committee chairman from 1966 to 1975. His theological thrust is clearly seen in the title of a book, *Revolution as Revelation*, by Sunand Sumithra.[9]

The Characteristics of the Biblical *Kairos*

The aberrations of the past must be a warning to us. They should induce us to examine carefully any claim that a special situation is God's appointed time. In most cases these claims reveal a new appearance of theological enthusiasm (*Schwärmerei*). We have, therefore, to ask three questions:

(1) What does the Bible teach about the nature of a divine *kairos*?

(2) Why is the present situation regarded as a special *kairos*, wholly different from former or coming seasons in history?

(3) How do the sponsors justify their identification of the present moment with the divine *kairos*?

Turning to the Bible, we find in relation to the first question that the word *kairos* is used in a positive way in connection with the unfolding of God's eternal plan of salvation. According to this plan, God has appointed special occasions in time and space when he would reveal himself, being always consistent with his own eternal decree. In such a *kairos* God comes near to man and causes an event in which his purpose of redemption is implemented by a new step, bringing the history of salvation closer to its conclusion—i.e., God's Kingdom in glory. The most significant use of the word *kairos* is found in Mark 7:15: "The time (the *Kairos*) is fulfilled, and the Kingdom of God is at hand; repent and believe in the gospel" (RSV). From this and similar statements we can conclude three aspects which are essential of a true *kairos*. These are:

(1) The chosen time comes through a free act of the sovereign God, an act in which man has no part and about which he can do nothing. In fact, God's appointed time is even contrasted to the so-called *kairoi* of human beings: "Your *kairos* is always," Jesus said to his natural relatives in John 7:6, thereby indicating the futility of their self-initiated undertakings. The *kairos* of God stands in even sharper contradiction to the opportune times of his human and satanic opponents. At his arrest Jesus said to the Jewish religious leaders who headed the mob, "But this is your moment, the time when Satan's power reigns supreme" (*The Living Bible*). It is

significant that here the evangelist (Luke 22:53) does not use the term *kairos*, but rather *hoora*, a more ambivalent term.

(2) God's *kairos* is centered in the sending of his Son, Jesus Christ, to implement his own plan of salvation to the world.

(3) In the present phase of God's dealing with mankind, God's *kairoi* are qualified in a *soteriological* way by his gracious actions. The purpose of God's *kairos* is to enable man to receive at the appointed moment, within the limited interval of a given time period, salvation, the forgiveness of sins, and the grace to become God's sons. Thus, by the gift of the Holy Spirit man is enabled to share in God's own divine nature.

If we now turn to the theological interpretation of the *kairos* given in the document itself, we find that none of these elements is genuinely contained in it.

First, the authors are unable to demonstrate that the *kairos* which they have in mind is really *initiated by God himself*. They do claim this, it is true, but what is their evidence? We shall return to this point soon.

Second, *Jesus Christ is in no way the center* of this *kairos*. In the decisive statements he is not even mentioned.

Third, the offer which, according to the authors, God is making has nothing to do with his redemptive grace. Instead, the opposite is true. In a most legalistic way *man is called to action* and the idea of reconciliation is rejected. Reconciliation is regarded as premature as long as political justice, according to the sponsors' own conception of justice, has not been achieved. In their opinion, such justice will come only by means of a hard struggle which will not be free from physical violence!

We must now consider our second guiding question: "In what way is the present situation different from other times in history?" The document tries to persuade us that the *tension* between the two classes in South African society, the oppressor and the oppressed, has reached its boiling point, its point of no return. If the claims of the oppressed are not met at once, they say, there will be a catastrophe. According to the authors, the same tension also divides the Church as such, placing two different churches in opposition to each other so that between the two no communion is possible. The question is whether this view has not been forced upon the situation. True enough, when the KD appeared in 1985 the racial conflict in South Africa was most serious and urgently called for a solution. Since, however, it had been like this for many years, the suspicion cannot be suppressed that some forces within and without South Africa were greatly interested in driving this tension by all means to the extreme. This would include a large-scale, armed conflict in order to reach their ultimate target. It is the decisive mark of *Marxist* ideology, clearly spelled out in the *Communist Manifesto* drawn up by Marx and Engels in 1848, to interpret history as a process of revolutionary struggle in which, finally, only two classes are opposed to each other—the exploiters and the exploited. The great turning point in history, the final victory of the international proletariat, will be that moment when the exploited will be fully conscious of their unbearable situation. Then they will take their destiny into their own hands and cast off their chains.

The radicalization of the South African crisis was not the outcome of a spontaneous development, nor was it the result of a drastic deterioration of the living conditions. It was not the result of the government's policy having become more brutal. On the contrary, the KD appeared at a time when effective reforms had been introduced already by the Botha government. Since then, the present Prime Minister, F. W. de Klerk, has achieved a most dramatic turn in South African politics, releasing the leader of the militant black opposition, Nelson Mandela, from prison, legalizing his African National Congress, and starting completely to dismantle the odious policy of *apartheid*. The hesitancy of KD proponents to acknowledge these changes betrays the sincerity or value of their attitude. At an ecumenical convocation in Seoul in March 1990, the general secretary of the South African Council of Churches, the Rev. Frank Chikane from Johannesburg, even warned the black opposition in his country to discontinue its armed resistance against the government.[10] This shows that the crisis spoken of in the KD, in spite of all attempts to resolve it, will not cease but will still increase by degrees as some ecumenically influential people try to use their influence to persuade people both inside and outside the country that only by continued pressure on South Africa and by a total revolution can a satisfactory new order be established.

This already answers our third question regarding the spiritual authority upon which the authors base their claim that this is a time when God is uniquely at work and has shown to them exactly what he wants to accomplish soon. During OT times, God at times raised up men, sometimes women, out of the midst of the people of Israel to whom, by special revelation, he communicated his purposes regarding his imminent and his future eschatological actions. The sponsors of the KD plead for a new, prophetic type of theology and present themselves as if they had received the gift of prophecy which enables them to perceive the will of God by reading the signs of the times.

They act in the same way as the staff members of the WCC in Geneva do when they try to impose their views upon reluctant member churches. They, too, claim a prophetic authority for their ministry. Nevertheless, what they and the sponsors of the KD are telling us can hardly be distinguished from the viewpoints propagated by other people in politics and journalism who do not even claim to be Christians. The "voice of prophecy" rendered by the KD was consonant with the contemporary worldwide battle cry that now the moment had come when the white minority government of South Africa must be brought to its knees and the present social system of the country must be overturned.

Certainly by that time most people had come to agree that effective change had to be introduced immediately. But the insight into such need was an expression of common sense and moral indignation rather than the answer to a special, divine revelation. If it had been the latter, its entire content would be compatible with the written record of God's previous self-disclosure in history—the Bible—and its teaching of God's way of salvation. But as to the KD, this is not the case, as we soon shall see. We have reason to suspect that the new *Kairos* Theology or rather *Kairos* ideology which expresses itself in a whole number of *Kairos* documents appearing now in different parts of the world where there is sociopolitical conflict must be discerned as attempts by some superhuman forces, acting inspirationally upon the minds of men, to assume increased control over the course of world history. These forces try to impose their rule upon human society in general, and on the Church of Jesus Christ in particular, by investing themselves with divine authority.

The NT calls these forces to which I refer the "*stoicheia tou kosmou,*" the elementary spirits of the created world. These spirits are part of the invisible world and were originally created to transmit God's will to the creation. They rebelled against the rule of God and tried, under the leadership of Satan, to set up their own dominion against God. We experience their influence in the formation of political empires and in the proclamation of totalitarian ideologies. If these are identified with the living voice of God, and if a total obedience is demanded in their name, then we are dealing with the very opposite to Christian prophecy. We are encountering a new manifestation of false prophecy.

It is quite interesting to note that the first affirmation and refutation of the famous Barmen Declaration of 1934[11] was specifically framed to counteract a similar false prophecy coming from those German Christians who identified National-Socialist ideology with a new *kairos,* a new dispensation from God. Its first affirmation stated: "Jesus Christ, to whom the Holy Scriptures testify, is the one Word of God, to whom we have to listen, and in whom we have to trust and obey in life and in death." Its first refutation states with equal firmness: "We reject, therefore, the false teaching that the Church can and must also recognise other events and forces, figures and truths as God's revelation besides this one Word of God."

I have the strong impression that the KD, indeed, is a manifestation of false prophecy which, if heeded, will prove fatal for the future of South Africa and its people, especially its churches. In order to maintain this charge, I have to substantiate it by a closer examination of the message of the KD as it is given first in negative and then in positive terms. It must then be compared with the biblical view of God's will for man both in his ordinances of preservation and his dispensations of salvation.

THE REJECTION OF BIBLICAL FAITH AND ITS IDEOLOGICAL SUBSTITUTION

We have dealt at some length with the methodological and episte-mological presuppositions of the KD, because at those very points the sponsors have set the fatal course which they follow through-out their document. This cannot be analyzed here in all its detail, but the distortion of Christian doctrine at the main stages of the KD must be indicated.

The Metaphysical Damnation of the Political Opponent

In the second chapter the sponsors wage an all-out attack on their main opponent, the present political system of South Africa. It is not an attack on the State as such, but rather on the underlying philosophical and moral foundation by which the system is upheld. It would have been expected that here an encounter with the ideol-ogy of *apartheid* or Separate Development would have been staged. We wonder why the authors have not chosen this theological avenue as other resisting churchmen have done many times before. Is the reason perhaps, as some critics have concluded, that the basic concern of the sponsors is no longer the *racial* issue as such, but that it has shifted to the socioeconomic realm? In the KD the enemy is not so much white *racism*, but rather *capitalism*, which allegedly uses the racial situation to strengthen the power of the ruling class against the social claims of the exploited majority, which happens to be non-white. In this case the authors could have enhanced their argument by discussing the inherent evils of the system of a free market economy and the advantages of a socialist order. The KD is, in fact, a thoroughgoing endorsement of the Marxist view of class struggle, and one of its sponsors, the Rev. Buti Tlhagale, has openly admitted that the authors have gleaned a lot from Marxist thought.

It goes without saying that it would have been self-defeating if the authors had presented a document in which the entire issue was stated in plain socioeconomic terms as a naked political power-struggle. Their aim is to win the *churches* for their cause and to persuade the *Christians* of its legitimacy, for they are aware of the strong grip the Christian faith still has on a considerable proportion of South Africa's population, both black and white. Therefore, the issue had to be presented as a problem of religious faith, and the argument had to be developed in theological terms.

We know from Latin America that the "Christians for Socialism" there are following a similar line in view of the seemingly unshakable strength of popular Catholicism. They are fighting the theoretical battle at the religious level. Their conscientization campaigns are appeals to the Christian sentiment, expressed in biblical language which is strangely blended with Marxist thought. This strategy, which can be traced in many pre-revolutionary situations all over the world, has been aptly named "Christo-Marxism."

We do not mean to insinuate that all sponsors of the KD are in reality adherents of a blatant Marxist (which means an atheistic) worldview and that they use the Christian faith only as a camouflage. However, we sadly gather from their very choice of words and from the appallingly hateful spirit pervading their paper that they have allowed Marxism to deeply penetrate their minds. In this process, their former biblical convictions have been affected and distorted to such a degree that they now are dedicating themselves to a syncretistic substitution for the genuine Christian faith. As seduced seducers, they now try to win others (if possible, the entire Church) for their new political religion.

This quasi-missionary campaign is first conducted in the controversial form of denouncing the religious convictions, whether genuine or simulated, of their political and ecclesiastical opponents. They do this because these convictions exercise a persuasive power on the minds and consciences of many Christians who maintain an attitude of loyalty or at least endurance over against the present political order.

The name given in the KD to the moral and religious legitimation of this order is "State Theology." Without presenting any documentary evidence that such a closed system of theological self-understanding of the present state really exists, the authors single out four elements of rather mixed nature which, according to their argument, constitute the main pillars of the alleged "State Theology." They then try to dismantle these conceptions one by one.

To begin, they take issue with the use of the Pauline treatment of the Roman government in the thirteenth chapter of his epistle to the Romans. The obedience demanded by Paul from the Christians in Rome to their imperial government is, as any reader can easily inform himself, based on the statement in verses 1 and 2, where we are taught that any ruling authority exists as an institution of God himself. Therefore, resisting such authority means that we resist God. If this is true, and for a Bible-believing Christian there is no alternative, then we have to obey even those governments we dislike. This includes communist dictatorships and, of course, also the present government formed by the National Party of South Africa. We obey such governments so far as their laws and rulings are not in clear opposition to the commandments of God; otherwise the *clausula Petri* would apply: "We must obey God rather than man" (Acts 5:19).

The KD, however, does not advocate the line of partial resistance. It wants the total removal of the present regime and the system on which it is based. Therefore, the authority of this scriptural passage is dissolved by declaring it as of situational relevance only. It was meant, they say, as a warning against an enthusiastic attitude which had been adopted by some Christians in Rome at that time who did not want to acknowledge any government whatsoever. However, the authors fail to give any exegetical evidence for such opinion. In actuality, it is only the arbitrary suggestion of two contemporary exegetes, O. Cullmann and E. Käsemann, to whom due reference is given. This is not convincing at all.

In order to strengthen their unyielding opposition to the present state, the authors criticize three further elements of "State Theology." The first is its insistence on law and order, which is dismissed with the allegation that it is misused as a defense of a system of injustice. The next pillar is its warning against the danger of a communist takeover. This risk is minimized with alarming ease as either being grossly exaggerated or as having been provoked by the present, oppressive system itself. Such an approach simply betrays the ideological sympathies of the sponsors of the KD!

The outrageous remarks under the final subheading, "The God of the State," cause even more dismay. Here the God invoked in the political statements of the South African regime is plainly denounced as an idol. He is characterized as "mischievous, sinister and evil." Finally, he is equated with "the very opposite of the God of the Bible," viz., the Devil, Satan and Antichrist.[12]

Now we do not want to exclude the possibility that there have been and still are cases where the authority of God has been called upon in a presumptuous way to defend and legitimize political activities and measures which are contrary to his holy will as revealed in the Bible. No Christian is exempt from this constant temptation to manipulate faith in God for one's own selfish purposes. In fact, the very group which makes this terrible accusation proceeds only a few pages later to commit the same sacrilege here attributed to their political opponents. They themselves, by assuming a prophetic role, identify their own ideological views and purposes, which they have admitted have been gleaned from the thought of Karl Marx, with a revelation they claim to have received from God himself.

Now Karl Marx was not just an agnostic or atheist. He was a declared enemy of God, and his entire ideology is an expression of anti-God Humanism in which man must take his destiny into his own hands and usurp God. In the KD document, the way of salvation for South Africa is called "the liberating mission of God and the church in the world," but this is indeed nothing other than the implementation of the Marxist-Leninist program of revolution which is to be carried out entirely by the people themselves. It does not alter this basically atheistic strategy when it is given a quasi-sacred appearance by its description as a "challenge that comes from God."

Now if the sponsors equate the God of the representatives of South Africa's state with Satan and Antichrist, they have passed upon those representatives more than a legal or moral judgment. They have, in fact, grouped them with the host of metaphysical demonic forces who can expect nothing other than the eternal fire which Jesus says is prepared for the Devil and his angels. In reaching such a conclusion, the sponsors deprive themselves of any opportunity to appeal to the Christian conscience of their opponents, many of whom, as is well known, stand in the tradition of revival-inspired, Reformed piety and are devout church members. Having read those dreadful lines, one can understand the attitude of some South African Christians who have said they could not tolerate the presence of this paper in their home because it seemed by a ghastly force to poison the entire atmosphere.

Yet the authors of the KD are not the first to have resorted to such an extreme discreditation of the spiritual integrity of the faith of their political opponents. We have similar statements from "Christians for Socialism,"[13] who accuse their opponents of worshiping idols, deities of death, metaphysical tyrants, and even the Devil instead of the true God of life. This alarming development confronts us with the possibility that the Church, not only in South Africa but all over the world, is threatened by a schism which is far more serious than the historic schism between Roman Catholicism and Protestantism. In fact, the final result could be the constitution of two different religions which are not merely incompatible, but are engaged in spiritual or even physical warfare with each other.

The Deliberate Polarization of the Church

The sponsors of the KD do not make any attempt to prevent such an irreparable cleavage within the South African Church. On the contrary, they proceed to do their utmost to speed up this polarization. The third chapter bears the title "Critique of Church Theology." The object of this chapter is to take issue with any theological position which tries to advocate a solution to the South African conflict in a peaceful rather than a revolutionary way. The attitude thus criticized is probably adopted by the majority of Christians, both white and non-white, although the readiness to engage in responsible ventures and personal sacrifices for the sake of preserving peace and promoting justice might exist in different degrees. This is surely the attitude of the majority of clear-sighted church leaders, as expressed in many statements both church-related or with political connections.

The authors rightly observe that in the thinking of such Christians, the term that figures most prominently is *reconciliation*, supplemented by the plea for *justice* and *nonviolence*. *Reconciliation*, which is a key concept in the biblical gospel, especially with St. Paul, and is related to *atonement*, would indeed be the Christian answer to the present conflict. This proposal is rejected outright by the KD. To its authors, reconciliation is applicable only in cases of conflict which are caused by personal dissension and misunderstandings which can be sorted out by calm negotiation. But there are other conflicts, they say—and they identify South Africa as one of them—that are nothing less than the struggle between justice and injustice, between good and evil, and—here comes the metaphysical judgment again!—between God and the Devil. In such a situation reconciliation is not possible, because it would be a conciliation with sin and the Devil.

Here, they say, a Christian has the duty not to plead for reconciliation without repentance. Rather, "like Jesus, we must expose this false peace, confront our oppressor and sow dissension."[14] It appears quite odd that here, on one of the few occasions when the name of Jesus is mentioned at all, it is cited in connection with a Christian's duty to sow dissension. Does this not mean that the whole gospel is turned upside-down in this document which claims to be a "Christian, biblical and theological comment on the political crisis in South Africa today"?[15]

It is true that the Bible does teach that true reconciliation with God and with our fellowmen involves repentance on the part of the sinner in order to remove the obstacle to true communion and fellowship. Jesus, however, interceded for those who crucified him before any of them had repented. This shows that we must forgive our adversaries in our heart even before they ask for forgiveness. Moreover, it is an entirely self-righteous attitude when one puts the entire blame on his opponent and claims all the justice for oneself. In that case, the relationship between the two equals the contrast between good and evil, between God and the Devil! It is also a gross presumption to equate one's political view about socioeconomic justice with the justice of God. Will the call for repentance, emanating from such a haughty attitude, ever reach the conscience of my guilty fellow Christians?

FINAL EVALUATION

It is quite obvious that a clear-sighted Christian has no other option but to reject this document as a perversion of the gospel. He must expose the seduction contained in it wherever unsuspecting Christians are inclined to accept its claim as a "challenge which comes from God." Our reason for doing so becomes even stronger when we realize that the document is not simply an expression of the personal convictions of some misguided people who happened to meet in Soweto. Rather, we should understand that it is an example of a modern, many-faceted ideology which, in Christian garments and with a partially traditional vocabulary, tries to hijack the Christian Church worldwide and to redirect its flight to an inner-worldly utopia. The KD is actually right when it points out that we are a divided Church, not only in South Africa but throughout the world. Yet, the dividing line does not run where the KD tries to draw it—i.e., between the political oppressors and the oppressed. Rather, it separates the sheep of the flock of Jesus Christ, who still recognize the authentic biblical voice of their Good Shepherd, from those who have lost their biblical sense of orientation—who are narcoticized by pseudo-Christian theologies and who therefore follow the hireling.

This, however, must not be considered as a reassuring endorsement of the political state of affairs in South Africa against which the sponsors of the KD were revolting. If our examination of the KD has forced us to refute it, we nevertheless must not do so with a self-assured or self-satisfied attitude. The fact that its sponsors are mistaken in their assessment of the South African crisis and have embarked on a disastrous course which would most probably lead to even sharper conflict and eventually to chaos, misery and tyranny should induce us to ask ourselves what traumatic experience might have caused them to be swayed by such fanaticism. Personally, I am fully convinced that the history of South Africa has both its bright and its gloomy aspects, although more and more it began to assume the character of a tragedy in the classical sense. (This tragedy has its origin in the chief actor—the white ruler— falling into sin, failing to recognize his guilt and make amends.)[16] At the same time, the white population of Dutch, British and other European stock has done much to develop the country, to introduce a high level of western culture and civilization, and also to assume a certain responsibility for the protection and welfare of the native and the imported non-white majority. Not to acknowledge this is an indication of blindness and unfairness.

Nevertheless, the white man was slow to recognize the true humanity of his black and colored fellowman. He developed an innate sense of superiority and treated the black man as his inferior who was predestined permanently to be kept in a second-class position and to receive only very limited rights in his own country. He was to serve the white master while at the same time suffering from an integral exclusion from his culture. The policy of *apartheid* assumed, indeed, features of a quasi-religious ideology which made very high moral claims, sometimes even under a sense of divine mission. At the same time it condoned the selfish interest of the white ruler who enforced this system on his black fellowman. Moreover, he was slow in the consistent implementation of the more constructive elements of *apartheid* policy.

I am also painfully aware of the many psychological injuries inflicted by inconsiderate white people on the minds of black people whose major disadvantage was their different color and their inferior social position. When the time had arrived to make some adjustment to this system and to allow the legitimate aspiration of the blacks to be met sympathetically and constructively, the white man refused to do so out of fear that this would undermine his present position and hazard his future. Thus, tension grew, and the conflict steadily assumed more dangerous dimensions. Still, the white man did not give in but increased the force to crush all resistance. This he did partly out of selfishness and partly out of a mistaken assessment of the seriousness of the situation. Above all, he was afraid that the black man would wreak a terrible revenge.

What can be the answer to such a seemingly hopeless situation? Common sense can see no hope in the extremes advocated by the radicals on either side. Neither can the course of revolution be adopted as the KD proposes; nor can the *status quo* be defended against the increasing opposition of the non-white majority within South Africa and its moral and material support from the outside world. Whether the middle way of the present de Klerk government, the way of resolute reforms to meet the legitimate claims of the black people and to protect the living rights of the white minority, will lead to success, I cannot answer with guaranteed assurance from a political point of view. It is, however, definitely worth trying, especially as there appears to be no political alternative.

Speaking as a Christian theologian, however, I definitely venture to say with confidence that there is a third way: *Reconciliation.* By this I do not mean a cheap type of shallow appeasement which is unmindful of the obstacles to such restoration of true fellowship. The word *reconciliation* is, as I stated before, a key term in the biblical doctrine of salvation. The reconciliation of which the NT speaks is the one which was secured on Calvary, where God himself gave his only Son as a sacrifice for the expiation of our sins. There he made peace between sinful mankind and himself. Out of such costly restoration of our broken relationship with God there proceeds the possibility of our being reconciled also with our estranged fellow human beings—if we approach each other in a humble spirit, ready to admit our own guilt and to forgive our fellowman in the name of Jesus Christ.

It is this message of reconciliation which proceeds directly from the cross, the message which Christ committed to his ambassadors, as Paul so wonderfully states: "God was in Christ, reconciling the world with Himself, not counting their trespasses against them and entrusting to us the message of reconciliation" (2 Cor 5:19).

The true *kairos* in the biblical sense is that opportune but limited time when God through his apostolic messengers makes his offer of reconciliation to a world that is dying under its sins and tensions and unresolved grievances. This acceptable time, the day of salvation, has not yet passed away, not even in suffering South Africa. God's offer is still valid. His divine Word, empowered by the Holy Spirit, still exercises its convicting force. I dare say there is still a fair amount of goodwill in the hearts and minds of people, both black and white, who have accepted this divine gift of atonement. Because of the Atonement, these people are longing to live by it both in their relationship to God and in their brotherhood with their fellow Christians of any color or social position. To them I want to plead:

Do not be frightened by the self-appointed prophets of doom and preachers of dissension, thereby becoming indifferent! Rather, make use of the acceptable time as long as God still lets his sun shine on good and evil people—in South Africa no less than in the rest of the world—the world he created and loved so much that he sacrificed his only begotten Son for it!

CHAPTER EIGHT

TEN CRITERIA TO DISCERN BETWEEN THE BIBLICAL KINGDOM AND ITS UTOPIAN COUNTERFEITS

We will now consider principles necessary in order to tell the true from the false, the genuine Kingdom of God from its counterfeits.

(1) The Kingdom of God has always been *the central motif of Christian missions* (cf. Mark 1:15; Matt 24:14), but in modern times this has become a blurred concept. Its biblical clarification is indispensable for the future of world evangelization.

(2) The Kingdom of God in its present reality and as an object of Christian hope can only be understood properly if we obediently consult God's promising and fulfilling self-disclosure in *the Scriptures*.

The Kingdom is bound to be misunderstood when it is unfolded according to human wishful thinking. This is the case even when contemporary secular experiences are used as the hermeneutical key to interpret the Scriptures, as is practiced largely in socio-critical exegesis and in socio-critical contextual theologies.

(3) God the Father has commissioned his Son to reestablish his reign over his corrupted creation. *Jesus Christ*, the Lamb of God,

has expiated the sins of the world by his sacrificial death. As the Risen One, he sends out his message of reconciliation in order to redeem people from rebellion, captivity and death and to lead them into his Kingdom and thereby into vital communion with God.

The redemptive reign of Christ is misunderstood in a "theology of liberation" which interprets his death on the cross not as the ground for the forgiveness of sins, but rather as an exemplary confrontation with historical powers in order to liberate the innocently suffering poor from captivity, and which assigns to them the rights of citizens in the Kingdom on account of their former exploitation.

(4) The Kingdom which is entrusted to the risen Christ takes its salvation-historical point of departure in *his Church*, which is gathered through evangelistic preaching to Israel and the Gentiles. The Church stands clearly *vis-a-vis* to the unbelieving world, but penetrates it as its salt and light through her witness in proclamation and service.

The Kingdom of God is misunderstood when the border between Church and world is erased and salvation history is identified with political history. This happens when mission is regarded essentially as a political function which is to contribute towards the emergence of a humane society.

(5) When believers submit to the messianic rule of Jesus, they also renounce the *satanic principalities and powers* who enslave unbelievers despite having been dethroned by the redemptive death of Christ.

This exorcizing dethronement is misunderstood in a "theology of liberation" which demythologizes biblical demonology and identifies those principalities and powers with repressive social power structures that are to be overthrown by political confrontation with or without violence.

(6) The task of mission is theologically determined by a clear distinction between the *Kingdom in grace* which already has arrived with Jesus of Nazareth and the *Kingdom in glory* which will arrive with his second coming. Mission mediates the spiritual gifts of the former through proclamation, sacraments and diaconate, while it

paves the way for the latter Kingdom through calling people into the decision of faith.

The eschatological orientation of mission is misunderstood in a process theology which expects the coming of the Kingdom as the logical result of history, irrespective of the personal return of Christ and the previous appearance of Antichrist in his counter-kingdom (2 Thess 2:3-10). Within such a misunderstanding, mission becomes overburdened by the task of constructing together with non-Christian movements the so-called Kingdom of God.

(7) According to the prediction of Jesus in Matt 16:3 and Luke 21:11-25, the coming of God's Kingdom can be recognized by the *signs of the time*. These consist negatively in the disruption of this old aeon by catastrophes in history, as well as in nature and in the growing harassment of the Church by false prophets and pseudo-messiahs. Positively, they consist in the proclamation of the gospel among all nations and finally in the conversion of Israel, God's ancient covenant people, to Jesus as her Messiah (Romans 11).

The signs of the coming Kingdom are misunderstood if they are identified with actions for sociopolitical change to be performed either by the Church or by non-Christian movements, even if such identification is done with reference to the signs which according to Christ's promise are to follow the preaching of his apostles (Mark 16:17-20).

(8) In the center of the biblical Kingdom stands *God the Father who saves through his Son and renews in the Holy Spirit*. The glorification of the Triune God in the new creation is the goal of the history of his Kingdom.

The Kingdom of God is misunderstood whenever the gospel of the Kingdom is perverted into an ideology that reinterprets God's saving grace as a legalistic action program for people and on behalf of people, and which falsifies God's promise of the eschatological revelation of his Kingdom as denoting a human utopia.

(9) The biblical statements concerning God's reign distinguish between his *preserving world dominion* through the agency of state authorities (Rom 13:1-6) and the execution of his plan of salvation through the *mission of the Church* of Jesus Christ (Matt 28:16-20).

God's reign is misunderstood when, by the identification of his preserving work and his salvific rule, the Church is politicized and forced into an ideological option.

(10) Biblical expectation of God's Kingdom finds its vital expression in the urge to *proclaim the gospel of the Kingdom amongst all nations* (Matt 24:14) until Christ comes again. The evangelization of the world is bound to collapse where the coming of God's Kingdom in power and glory is not expected with the return of the Lord, but is rather associated with our involvement for a new world order in which political power and economic wealth are redistributed and where such involvement is declared to be our new assignment in world mission.

CHAPTER NINE

MARTYRDOM—GATE TO THE KINGDOM OF HEAVEN

A mong the various great religions, it is Christianity that has set forth martyrdom as an expression of its faith. This expression is so important that there has never been a Christian generation which did not add another purple page to the dramatic chronicle of martyrs, gaining thereby an existential insight into martyrdom's deep spiritual significance for the life of the Church. The Latin Church Father St. Augustine once wrote:

> From Abel until the end of this age the pilgrim church proceeds between the persecutions of the world and the consolations of God.[1]

For St. Augustine, the time of the Church begins, we note, with the sons of our first parents and lasts until the conclusion of the history of this fallen world. From her origin to her perfection, it is central to the very nature of the faithful Church to be hated and persecuted by the world. The Church cannot be the Church and can never reach her eschatological destination in the Kingdom of glory if she does not accept this calling but rather shuns suffering and tries to reach a peaceful arrangement with an ungodly world. I am afraid that a large section of world Christianity is in severe danger of losing sight of this truth. Therefore, the purpose of this final chapter is to remind my readers of a very elementary but costly truth about the connection between the Church on earth and the Kingdom of Heaven.

PART I: MARTYRDOM BELONGS TO THE NATURE OF CHRIST'S CHURCH

When Jesus called his first disciples to follow him, he allowed them initially to witness a certain period of marvelous events. They heard his powerful preaching about God's Kingdom that attracted thousands of people who listened with amazement to him. They saw his mighty signs that convinced them Jesus was no ordinary person but the expected Messiah who acted with the authority of God.

However, at the very moment that Peter expressed this faith in his historic confession, "Thou art Christ, the Son of the living God," Jesus suddenly changed the apparent course of events. He did not confirm contemporary Jewish messianic expectations that he would liberate Israel from all suffering and oppression. Instead, he confided a painful secret to his disciples which they found inconceivable and to which they reacted in horror. This was true especially of Peter who cried, "God forbid, Lord. This shall never happen to you." What was the shocking information that nearly turned Peter away from being a confessor and made him instead a tempter, a Satan, as Jesus called him? It was the disclosure that Jesus, according to God's mysterious providence, had to go to Jerusalem and suffer many things at the hands of the elders and chief priests and even be killed. Jesus revealed to them that his present ministry would not be crowned with great earthly success, but that he would have to die before his final triumph—life out of death—would be accomplished. Moreover, this would be not only *his* fate, but his followers would have to accept the same destiny. They would have to take up their own crosses and follow him on the road to Calvary. They must be ready to lose their lives for his sake in order to find them (Matt 16:24f.).

Jesus had to repeat this hard lesson several times before the disciples could grasp and accept it. But in doing so, he did not present this instruction as a mere inconceivable law. No, he proceeded to uncover for them the reason his disciples must willingly accept hatred and persecution as their unavoidable lot:

> "If the world hates you, know that it has hated me before it hated you. If you were of the world the world would love its own; but because you are not of this world, but I chose you out of the world, therefore the world hates you. Remember the word that I said to you, 'a servant is not greater than his master.' If they persecuted me, they will persecute you; if they kept my word, they will keep yours also. But all this they will do to you on my account because they do not know him who sent me" (John 15:18-21).

Behind the hatred of the world stands the primeval hatred of the prince of this world who rebelled against God. He wants to subdue this world to his rule. He knows, however, that this usurped position is going to be taken away from him by God's own Son, whom God has appointed to be the Redeemer and real Ruler of the world. Satan reacts to this in fury! His hatred is directed primarily against Jesus Christ himself. He wants to crush him in order to prevent his work of redemption from taking place. But he cannot succeed in this, so his wrath turns against the followers of Christ. They still live in this world; they are sent into it in order to bring all nations under the authority of Christ by proclaiming to them the gospel of his atoning death and glorious resurrection. Therefore, they become the new target of Satan's fierce attacks.

The disciples were very soon to experience the truth of Christ's prediction. In the early chapters of the Acts of the Apostles, we read of the persecutions that immediately after the establishment of the Church were directed against the apostles because of their fearless witness to Christ's resurrection. We read about Stephen, the first Christian martyr, who was to lead the long line of future martyrs whose names were to be written in the honorable chronicle of the Church militant. The Christians accepted this, and amongst the first instructions which the early missionaries gave their converts was the warning, "through many tribulations we must enter the Kingdom of God" (Acts 14:22).

Paul admonished the young Christians not to be scandalized by watching his own sufferings in consequence of his ministry. In his epistles we find several catalogues of his internal and external tribulations which he had endured and which he regarded as the normal fate of a Christian warrior. At the same time he saw in those tribulations a confirmation of the truth of his message, which he would not deny under any pressure or circumstances.

The NT writings also contain the conviction that in the future such persecution would increase. In fact, the closer the time of the witnessing Church draws to its completion, and the nearer the day of our final redemption draws through the glorious return of Christ, the sharper will be the attacks of the demonic adversary. He will try to shake the faith of Christians and to divert their loyalty from their heavenly Master.

In Jesus' great eschatological sermons on the Mount of Olives and in the book of Revelation, persecutions appear as an apocalyptic feature. They are the experience of the final battle between the opposing kingdoms of Christ and the Antichrist in which, alas, many lukewarm Christians will despair. This, however, will culminate in the visible return of Christ, the destruction of Antichrist, and the establishment of Christ's Kingdom in power and great glory.

What Jesus had foretold to his disciples was experienced by them in many individual and corporate persecutions. Under Nero, two of the chief apostles—Peter and Paul—lost their lives. Whenever Christian missionaries entered a new cultural territory to claim it for their Lord, the traditional religious and political authorities saw their power endangered. They therefore turned in enmity against both the foreign messengers and their indigenous converts. There is no single national church and no generation that has been spared such fiery trials. This is recorded in every textbook of mission history.

But one pathetic fact is much less known even amongst Christians, and that is that *our twentieth century is the bloodiest in the entire history of Christianity*. Never since the time of Christ's birth have so many persecutions of Christians taken place as in our day. A broad tract of blood leads through Armenia, Ethiopia, Uganda, Korea, Vietnam and other totalitarian states. During the first two decades of this century one of the oldest churches, the Armenian Church, had to endure heavy attacks. During the years 1915-1918, 1.5 million Armenians were butchered, one of the most horrible genocides in history. In Germany, under Adolf Hitler, both Protestants and Catholics who actively resisted his totalitarian Nazi ideology were put into concentration camps, and several of them were martyred.

The heaviest blood toll, however, was and still is demanded by states which give their ideological allegiance to Marxist Socialism or Communism. It is an undeniable fact that in all Marxist-ruled countries the Church has been or still is, to different degrees, subjected to hostility and attack. Open persecution may relax at times, either because it appears opportune to the government to do that or because the churches have yielded to the pressure and have entered into compromises. Yet the declared goal of the Marxist state remains the same: to subdue and eliminate the Christian religion.

We have to realize that anti-Christian acts by communists are not simply expressions of the irresponsible display of brutal power inherent in any totalitarian system. Rather, we have to remember that hatred for the Christian faith lies at the very root of Marxism-Leninism. As a schoolboy, Marx had a loving faith in God. But as a university student, he turned suddenly against God in an enmity which was metaphysically inspired. Consequently, in the introduction to his dissertation he wrote: "The confession of Prometheus— 'I hate all gods'—is its (philosophy's) own confession . . . against all heavenly or earthly gods that do not recognise man's self-consciousness as the supreme godhead. . . ."[2]

Similarly, Vladimir Lenin hated religion and in particular the Christian Church. From his youth and out of the depths of his soul, he called himself a "personal enemy of God." In 1909 he wrote: "We have to fight against religion. This is the ABC of Materialism and thus, consequently, of Marxism too. . . ."[3] Even today, therefore, the Communist Party of the Soviet Union is duty-bound, according to Article 6 of the new constitution of 1977, to "struggle against religious prejudice."

The reason all convinced Marxists hate Christianity is the same. The gospel claims that Jesus Christ is the only way for the redemption of mankind in his coming heavenly Kingdom. This constitutes a direct contradiction of the Marxist claim that by following his materialistic ideology man will be able in his own strength to erect the so-called "Kingdom of Freedom," the classless society.

The first church which under Communism was to undergo a terrible outrage of anti-Christian hatred was the Russian Orthodox Church. Since the famous October Revolution, it has been subjected to a persistent chain of persecutions which has gradually affected also the other churches in the expanding Soviet empire. We do not have space to trace the terrible history of persecutions in the Soviet Union from the first outburst of brutality during the years 1918-1922 when ten thousand bishops, priests and monks were executed and thousands of churches, monasteries and seminaries were destroyed, vandalized or dedicated to secular and even anti-religious functions. The Lutheran Church in the Baltic states experienced a similar fate. In 1937, the Lutheran Church in Estonia had 850,000 members, of whom 250,000 later emigrated. The 1981 census showed a remaining active church membership of only 60,742 practicing Christians.

The struggle of the unregistered evangelical Baptists to live their faith without yielding to the unacceptable legal restrictions on their religious rights has been particularly made known through the sufferings of the family of Georgi Vins. The death of Brezhnev did not result in any lessening of the pressures upon believers. On the contrary, the Alliance of Emigré Evangelical Baptist Churches in Germany several years ago informed the public about their fellow Christians in Russia and the renewed problems they were then facing. Under the government of Andropov our brethren experienced the harshest measures which had been taken against churches of any denomination in many years.

The history of Christian martyrdom is indeed a pathetic one.

A prospect of no end of anti-Christian persecution being in sight in the world is surely frightening. Yet if we look only at the atrocities of the enemies of the faith and at the pains endured by believers, we have seen merely one side of the picture given to us in the quotation from St. Augustine. In order to see martyrdom in its true perspective, we must also look at it from the other side and speak of *the consolations of God.*

PART II: MARTYRDOM BRINGS GREAT BLESSING TO CHRIST'S CHURCH

A Christian's natural reaction to the prospect of suffering will normally be one of anxiety and a desire to escape, as we saw in the case of Peter. But when Jesus announced to his disciples the divine necessity for his and their suffering, he did not stop at the painful prospect. Neither did he ever interpret such suffering as a tragedy. For him persecution was no proof of failure. In immediate connection with his announcement he spoke also of the glorious outcome of the atoning death of the Son of Man: ". . . and on the third day he will rise again!" (Matt 16:21).

The death of Christ is the divinely appointed pathway to his never-ending triumphant joy. The same also applies to the members of his body, the Church. For them, too, suffering and death for Christ's sake are part of their transition into everlasting life and joy. This joy does not begin only when their tribulations have ceased. It emerges during their afflictions, although its source remains hidden to the world. God's consolations, of which St. Augustine speaks, are experienced against the dark background of our present grief.

The secret of Christian suffering for the sake of the faith is that it unites us deeply to Jesus Christ, who is the source of our true life. The apostles regarded their afflictions as a privilege, and they taught their church members to see theirs likewise. In this way they proved to be worthy followers of their Lord, who himself became God's suffering servant. In such affliction, a close fellowship was constituted between Christ and the believers and also with the apostles who were their fathers and forerunners in the faith. From his prison in Rome Paul wrote to the Philippians: "For it has been granted to you that for the sake of Christ you should not only believe in him but also suffer for his sake, engaged in the same conflict you saw and now hear to be mine" (Phil 1:29f.). From NT times until the present, Christians' experience has been that Christ is never so consciously close to them as when they are conformed to him in their trials. David Yang, a Chinese martyr under Mao, wrote out of his own painful experience:[4]

> The Lord's heart is so much filled with compassion that he cannot have pleasure at the sight of his suffering children. But in order that we grow inwardly, that we reach spiritual maturity and become conquerors, he sometimes delays our liberation. He sustains us with the power of endurance until the end so that we obtain the crown of glory. The faith that is tried by fire is more precious than refined gold.

It is the crucified and risen Lord to whom Christians are united in martyrdom, and when they accept a share in his dying for our sake, they also experience the power of heavenly life which resurrected him from the dead. The new man, who is restored to the image of God, is created in us spiritually at our new birth. He is still hidden and must grow to live in place of our old nature until the day of our resurrection when we will be revealed as true children of God at the glorious appearing of Jesus Christ, our firstborn brother. This hidden, new man in us is strengthened mightily and made to grow just when our psycho-physical nature is thrown into a process of affliction: "Though our outer nature is wasting away, our inner nature is renewed every day. For this slight momentary affliction is preparing us an eternal weight of glory beyond all comparison" (2 Cor 4:16). At the moment of our apparent breakdown, the regenerating power of resurrection takes proper effect in us. We experience Christ's defeat of death, and in the midst of all afflictions Christ makes us more than conquerors (Rom 8:37).

It is reported not only of Stephen but of several of the blood martyrs of the ancient Church that in the moment of dying they saw the risen Lord calling them to his heavenly glory. Although such visions are extraordinary blessings, we nevertheless can be assured that Christ is specially near to all his suffering brethren. He imparts to them a degree of sustaining grace which surpasses all blessings we receive through the means of grace under normal conditions.

Such strengthening under suffering for Christ's sake is given not only for the sake of the afflicted Christian himself. Endurance of pain and even death is at the same time a mighty endorsement of the truth of our testimony. The word *martyr* means "witness." Witnesses are called in connection with court trials to give evidence and to help establish the real circumstances surrounding an event about which the contesting parties hold opposing views and about which they give conflicting accounts. In the book of Isaiah (43:9f.), the conflict between Israel's faith and the religion of her pagan neighbors is depicted in a metaphorical court case between Israel's God, Jahweh, and the pagan idols. In this trial God wants to establish the truth that he alone is God, the sole Ruler of history and Creation. Jahweh, therefore, calls his chosen people, Israel, to be his witnesses. Out of their own experience of God's mighty acts of redemption, they are to provide the evidence that they found miraculous salvation in him alone.

Likewise, Jesus calls his apostles to be his witnesses (Acts 1:8). They are to preach his gospel not only as a set of doctrines and moral rules but as divine realities. They have experienced the transforming power of Christ's death and resurrection in their own lives. The very boldness with which these plain men dared to speak in front of the hostile Jewish authorities was a most impressive fact that added greatly to the attraction of their faith. But this convicting force was even increased when the Jewish and pagan world saw their readiness to sacrifice their lives as an endorsement of their witness. In view of their impending death, their final words spoken to their prosecutors assumed a sacred dignity that impressed everyone deeply. In some cases this persuaded the persecutors to themselves embrace the faith of their victims! These testimonies were remembered by their fellow Christians, written down in the chronicles of their martyrdom, and read in the Christian assembly as a source of strength, even for future generations. Tertullian gave expression to a universal experience of the Early Church when he coined the famous statement: "*Sanguis martyrorum est semen ecclesiae*"— "The blood of the martyrs is the seed of the Church."

The example of those ancient Christian martyrs has found a remarkable repetition in the experience of persecuted Christians in our time, especially those in the Soviet Union. They, too, discovered there is no better situation in which to become evangelizing witnesses than when they are taken into the courtroom in order to answer the cross-questioning of their judges. We know of many instances where these martyr Christians spent much time and were extremely diligent in the preparation of their plea to the jury. They did not plead for mercy or lenience. Rather, they tried to utilize the situation to embrace a unique opportunity to preach the gospel to an influential atheistic audience. Some evangelical prisoners even cast their speeches for their defense into the form of poems. These were stenographed by their friends and printed by the *Samizdat* underground press as a source of spiritual strength for their likewise endangered fellow Christians.

When in 1966 Georgi Vins was about to receive his first sentence of imprisonment for ten years followed by deportation, he recited before his judges a poem from which I quote the following verses:[5]

Not for robbery, nor for gold
Do we stand before you.
Today, here, as in Pilate's day,
Christ our Saviour is being judged.

No! you cannot kill the freedom of belief
Or imprison Christ in gaol!
The examples of his triumphs
Will live in hearts He's saved.

We call upon the Church of Christ
To tread the path of thorns;
We summon to a heavenly goal,
We challenge perfidy and lies.

Fresh trials now and persecution
Will serve alone to strengthen faith
And witness God's eternal truth
Before the generations still to come.

As we have seen so far, martyrdom has a great meaning for the spiritual upbuilding of every believer and for the Church's witness to the world. At the same time, martyrdom also has an ecclesiological function: It gives a deeper dimension to the brotherhood of all Christians. The mutual loyalty of Christians going through similar trials is encouraging. Together they make discoveries of hidden truths in the revealed Word of God, truths of which the Church had formerly only a shallow perception. What is really important in our doctrinal traditions is often found out only in situations where our faith is put on trial and we are asked to give account for the hope which is in us. That which is so precious to a believer that he risks his freedom and even his life rather than give it up will not easily be dismissed as merely ornamental. Rather, it will be made subject to a new investigation of its abiding spiritual significance. I have never heard of a single Christian who became a martyr for a so-called "demythologized" gospel, stripped by rationalistic minds of its transcendental foundation.

I am also convinced that the true solution of the ecumenical problem will not be found by mere theological debates, nor by sociopolitical action programs which demand no particular religious faith but might even be motivated by ideological utopias. A real mutual understanding of Christians from different confessional traditions, however, is gradually being reached in our time in concentration camps where Catholic, evangelical and Orthodox believers have to suffer for the same basic convictions. There they celebrate their common faith by worshiping together, and they also share what is dear to them in their own particular traditions. In his *Samizdat* publication "The Voice of the Apostate,"[6] S. Denisov tells us that those who have fallen away from the faith must undergo, before they reenter the Church, a period of public penitence. This penitence consists in forming small, new fraternities and praying together that the Church may find its unity again. "We firmly hope to become part of that One Christian Church which takes to her motherly bosom all members of the sects, the orthodox, the Protestant and the Catholic. Only by joining all God's loving forces can the battle be won." M. Meerson-Aksenov writes in his book *The People of God and the Shepherd* (1972):

> The forces of hell cannot destroy the Church in her wholeness. But which self-centered confession that opposes the others dares to claim for itself such fulness? When the Lord founded his church, did he say that her fragments will be isles of freedom?

Finally, the discovery of the wholeness of the Church also means rediscovering the important links between the militant, the suffering, and the triumphant Church. When we confess the communion of saints, we should remind ourselves that the body of Christ embraces as its members not only the Christians of our own generation but also those believers who have already finished their course. This testimony, too, can be a divine consolation for the pilgrim Church. We are, indeed, surrounded by a great cloud of witnesses (Heb 12:1). The testimony of Peter, Paul and John, the testimony of Perpetua and Felicitas, the testimony of John Hus and Thomas Cranmer, and the testimony of the Ugandan martyrs still speaks to the Church today. The testimony of Maximilian Kolbe and of Ivan Vasiljewitsch Moisejev, that Russian soldier who in July 1972 was tortured and drowned in the Black Sea because, undaunted, he preached and defended his faith, is still heard by the Church of Jesus Christ today.[7] These witnesses exhort us even in our hardest trial never to throw away our confidence which has a great reward (Heb 10:35). The last message that Ivan Moisejev sent to his friends concluded with the eschatological promise given to the martyr church in Smyrna (Rev 3:11): "Hold fast what you have so that no one may seize your crown."

I hope we now realize the great significance martyrdom has for the spiritual health and growth of Christ's Church. But what have we who at present are not persecuted to observe so that such blessing may take effect in the whole Church of Christ today?

PART III: MARTYRDOM CALLS FOR THE UNFAILING SOLIDARITY OF CHRIST'S CHURCH

The Pauline understanding of the Church as one body implies a close interdependence between all Christians. An event that deeply affects one member will necessarily concern all other members. Paul states: "If one member suffers, all suffer together; if one member is honored, all rejoice together" (1 Cor 12:26). The first condition for this corporate participation in joy and in suffering is, of course, a lively communication between the members. It can, however, be difficult if they are physically separated by political barriers set up to prevent such interaction. For a long time this has been the fate of the oppressed Christians in the Soviet Bloc states. Happily, not even the Iron Curtain was able to cut all lines of communication. During the time of suppression many channels were dug through which news and petitions could be passed on to us and effective aid sent to them. Outstanding work was done by organizations such as Faith in the Second World in Zürich or Keston College in Great Britain, which provided us with scientifically established information. Special relief agencies were formed for channeling material support to our fellow Christians. Institutions such as *La Voix de l'Orthodoxie* ventured to broadcast spiritual nurture to our starving fellow believers. Organizations such as the International League of Human Rights, Christian Solidarity International, and Amnesty International courageously brought cases of violated human rights to the knowledge of the public and pleaded the cause of the oppressed before international secular and religious forums.

We also received most authentic descriptions and analyses of the spiritual situation in eastern countries by persons who were leading spokesmen of the dissenters' movements but who were later sent into exile in the West. In such cases exile was either at their own request or forced upon them by the State. The names of Alexander Solzhenitsyn, Vladimir Maximov, and Tatiana Goritsheva are symbolic of this whole choir of voices that have been trying to alert the Christians in the democratic West to the growing communist suppression of freedom and also to the unexpected spiritual renewal that has gone on in Soviet Russia despite such suppression.

How did churches and individual Christians in the West react to such information and urgent requests for support? Here we face the scandalous fact that only a responsible minority showed any sign of active concern. The agencies for mission and relief in eastern countries managed to attract their faithful supporters, it is true, and certain democratic institutions did have the courage to champion the cause of persons whose rights are encroached upon in contradiction of the Act of Helsinki. But in contrast to this, the majority of our western denominations and their local churches showed very little response to the suffering of our fellow Christians in socialist countries in Eastern Europe. The same, unfortunately, is still true concerning areas of persecution in Asia and Africa. Despite the abundance of reliable information made available to us, very little of it appears in official religious news services and church papers. Our persecuted brethren urgently plead that we intercede for them. Such intercession, however, mentioning names and concerns, is virtually absent from the worshiping life of most congregations even though lists with detailed topics for intercession are sent freely to the pastoral offices.

The same indolence has been practiced for a long time by the Church at large as it is represented by the WCC. I vividly remember a most dramatic episode which I witnessed during the Assembly in Nairobi in 1975.[8] Two outstanding campaigners for religious liberty in the Soviet Union, the Russian Orthodox priest Gleb Jakunin and the layman Lev Regelson, had managed to get an open letter to the Assembly, smuggled through the Iron Curtain. In it they appealed to the ecumenical delegates to voice a public protest against the violation of religious freedom in their country, which they described in detail. Since the WCC, despite many appeals, had up to then observed silence with regard to these conditions in the Soviet Union, the appeal called upon them to inform all Christians on a regular basis about the fate of their fellow believers wherever they are persecuted in the world. As soon as this letter was published in the East African paper *Target*, both official delegations from the Soviet Union—the representatives of the Moscow Patriarchate and those of the All Union Council of Baptists—denounced the letter. They even questioned the moral integrity of its authors. When the Swiss delegate Dr. Jaques Rossell tried to place the matter of religious liberty in the Soviet Union on the agenda of the Assembly, the two Russian Orthodox Metropolitans Philareth and Nicodim protested so forcefully that the Assembly finally resolved not to debate the issue, but rather to ask the General Secretariat in Geneva to investigate the matter. It was supposed to investigate the respect for religious liberty in all signatory states of the Helsinki Act and then to report its findings to the Central Committee. A small confidential consultation was held in Montreux, Switzerland, but in his report to the Central Committee in August 1976 the general secretary, Philip Potter, spoke in very general and formal terms. He did not mention a single example of violated religious freedom in eastern countries.

As a matter of fact, from the time the churches of the Eastern European countries were accepted as members of the WCC in New Delhi in 1961 until the recent dramatic collapse of the Iron Curtain due to Michail Gorbachev's policy of *détente*, never did the Council dare to boldly denounce the violation of human rights—including religious liberty—in communist states. There were several reasons for this:

First, the WCC was afraid that such intervention might cause these eastern churches to resign from membership. The WCC did not take into account, however, that the leaders and delegates of these churches did not really speak on behalf of their members, but rather were acting on the instructions of their communist governments, as least in matters relating to politics. Therefore, the persecuted Christians actually felt betrayed by their own leaders and tended to form their own underground communities.

The second reason, however, has been that the political philosophy cherished by most staff members and accredited advisers of the WCC is a radical Socialism which has much sympathy with

Marxist social analysis. The ecumenical authorities have tended to treat Marxism as an ally against those political and economic systems which the WCC regards as the main causes of human oppression—e.g., western capitalism and white racism. This rather simplistic and one-sided view has often caused blindness to the even greater evils which are created by Marxist Socialism—e.g., in Eastern Europe, Ethiopia or Vietnam. The WCC has always gone into great detail to expose and actively combat actual or alleged offenses in countries of southern Africa, Latin America, and even of the entire NATO Alliance. By its special funds for its Programme to Combat Racism (PCR), it has even supported Marxist guerrilla movements in southern Africa which raided mission stations and after gaining governmental power started to encroach upon the liberty of Christian churches. In the same year (1970) that the PCR began, the WCC also inaugurated a Program for Dialogue with Other Religions and Ideologies. But it has never contemplated starting a program to combat anti-Christian ideologies that dehumanize the lives of whole peoples who desire simply to live according to their Christian convictions. I do not advocate special funds to support prospective freedom fighters in Marxist countries. The Church should always confine herself to using the sword of the Spirit, which is the Word of God. But it should use it fearlessly, prophetically and impartially, to the left as much as to the right.

Geneva argued that in certain delicate situations a cautious pleading with totalitarian governments can achieve more to alleviate the suffering of individuals than a dramatic public denunciation. This is true to some extent, although the Russian dissenters were calling for another course of action.

A similar line of caution was followed by the Lausanne Committee, which did not want to endanger its supporters in communist countries. This policy stood, however, in open contrast to the spiritual position laid down in the Lausanne Covenant of 1974, for Paragraph 13 says in quite unambiguous terms: "We also express our deep concern for all who have been unjustly imprisoned, and especially for our brethren who are suffering for their testimony to the Lord Jesus. We promise to pray and work for their freedom. . . ." Happily enough the Congress Lausanne II in Manila brought a significant improvement by giving clear prominence to the testimony of our brethren and sisters in areas of restriction and oppression in such nations as Nepal and China.

CONCLUSION

I have tried to show that demonstration of solidarity is necessary not only for the sake of the most afflicted members of Christ's body, but that it at the same time opens up channels through which the particular blessings received by them in their trials are used to revive the other members of Christ's body. A Church that forsakes her martyrs, that neither prays nor fearlessly cares for them, not only disturbs the spiritual communion between all members of Christ's body, but will eventually betray Christ himself, the Head of the body, who still suffers with his members. To his needy followers and members Jesus said:

> "Truly I say to you, as you did it to one of the least of these my brethren, you did it to me. . . . As you did it not to one of the least of these, you did it not to me" (Matt 25:40, 45).

Let us become more mindful of the eternal consequences which our Lord attributed to such action or inaction on behalf of the least of his brethren! Our spiritual identification with those suffering for Christ's sake and our readiness to face persecution ourselves deeply unite us with him in his reign of grace now and strengthen our hope that we together with them will share in his reign of glory. For he himself says:

> "Blessed are those who are persecuted because of righteousness, for theirs is the kingdom of heaven" (Matt 5:10).

WORLD MISSIONS FOLLOWING SAN ANTONIO AND MANILA 1989

Statement of the European Convention of Confessing Fellowships at Its Meeting in Frankfurt, March 1990

INTRODUCTION

Twenty years ago, on March 4, 1970, the Theological Convention of Confessing Fellowships published its widely acclaimed "Frankfurt Declaration on the Fundamental Crisis of Missions." At its 44th meeting, March 6-8, 1990, the Theological Convention addressed itself anew to a theological understanding of Christian world-mission in the modern age, for the following three reasons:

First of all, the Convention wanted to reflect upon and to reconsider that earlier event and what lay behind it. Secondly, it appeared necessary to the Convention to clarify the concept of mission in the light of various projects for increased missionary endeavor at the approach of the third millennium. Thirdly, the Convention was spurred on by two international conferences which have given new impetus to world mission in the past year [1989]. The first of these was the World Missions Conference sponsored by the World Council of Churches, held in San Antonio, Texas, May 21-31; the other was the Second International Congress for World Evangelization, convened by the evangelical Lausanne Movement and held in Manila (Philippines) July 11-20.

In reflecting upon these conferences, we were guided especially by the question, whether the fundamental crisis of world mission, as indicated by us in 1970, had in the meantime been resolved. Is there perhaps a growing theological consensus between the two mission movements, at that time so divergent, a consensus which may promise future cooperation and eventual unification? In response to this key question the European Convention of Confessing Fellowships was led to present the following statement of its position.

I. CONCERNING THE RESULTS FROM SAN ANTONIO

A. What Awakened Evangelical Hopes

1. Not since the Willingen Conference of 1952 had biblically-minded participants of such a congress been able to bring in significant scriptural statements about the content and goal of mission, and that even in the first of the four sectional reports ("Turning to the Living God"). Particularly important here are the references to the Triune God as the Author and Sustainer of the mission of the Church, to God's merciful disposition to us in Jesus Christ, the crucified and risen Lord and Saviour, as well as to the commission of the Church to present a united witness to God's reconciling love in Him.

2. That the biblical understanding of salvation was able to get a hearing at this juncture was primarily due to the fact that the drafting of this Sectional Report was done by an evangelical theologian, Professor David Bosch. Numerous representatives of the

Orthodox Churches, especially the Greek missiologist Bishop Anastasios of Androussa,[1] exhibited the same spirit.

3. The attention drawn by Bishop Lesslie Newbigin to the special challenge which the secularization of the modern world poses to Christian mission—a point not included in the official agenda—was specially welcomed by evangelical participants as a necessary admonition to the Geneva Ecumenical Movement that it should address anew the question, "How can the West be converted?"

B. What Still Challenges Us to Be on Our Guard

1. In San Antonio the former director of the WCC Division for World Mission and Evangelism, Dr. Eugene Stockwell, and his successor, Dr. Christopher Duraisingh, clearly displayed their openness to a new understanding of salvation in social and political terms and to Utopian ideas of a renewed world-order.[2]

2. Above all they posited an alleged saving revelation of God in the non-Christian religions as well. They arrived thereby at such offensive statements as "Jesus is the only way by which most of us have found the way to God. . . . But in our encounters with people of other faiths we cannot deny that many of them have a profound relationship with God."[3] This is a direct contradiction of the statement of Jesus in John 14:6, "No one comes to the Father, but by me," as well as of the basic apostolic message in Acts 4:12, "There is salvation in no one else. . . ."

3. The report of Section II ("Participating in Suffering and Struggle")—set alongside the Section I report as having equal importance—brings to light a massive social-revolutionary reversal of the message of Christ. Derived from this is a political commission to the disciples of Jesus "to join with the oppressed in the struggle for the transformation of society."[4] The commission of Jesus, according to Matt. 28:18-20, stands fundamentally opposed to this.

4. In the same Section the "Intifada," the Arab revolt against Israeli sovereignty, is described uncritically as "an authentic mani-

festation of the creative power" (of the church).[5] In contrast to this partisanship for the Palestinians, the key significance of Israel in the saving purpose of God (Rom. 9-11!) was not mentioned at all.

5. The Section I report commends the "Conciliar Process" which, like the New Age Movement, has as its goal a world which is politically, economically and religiously unified.[6]

6. For the first time at an ecumenical conference on mission representatives of other religions were invited to San Antonio, not just as observers, but also as consultants. In the sections and in the plenary sessions they participated fully in the conversation.

7. We recognize that there were in San Antonio some good insights and worthy individual contributions. But to our sorrow, because of the points we have listed above, we are not able to identify any change of direction in the Geneva Department for World Mission and Evangelism. Those in charge are obviously continuing to follow the course set since Uppsala (1968), with which we first took issue in our Frankfurt Declaration of 1970.

C. The "Bridge-building" of Some Evangelicals Was Premature

1. In an attempt at bridge-building, a group of about 160 participants at the San Antonio Conference "representing evangelical concerns" signed an Open Letter to the impending Lausanne Congress in Manila.[7] The letter contains a report of their "many good experiences" at the ecumenical conference. It also makes a plea for an acknowledgement of the social and political involvement of the World Council of Churches, and recommends, on the basis of an alleged "consensus" between "Ecumenicals" and "Evangelicals," that the Geneva Commission on World Mission and the Lausanne Movement hold their next world conference in partial cooperation, at the same time and in the same place.

2. In the light of the results from San Antonio the European Conference of Confessing Fellowships is not able to share the concerns and the viewpoint of this Letter. For this reason it expresses

its appreciation to the Lausanne Executive Committee for not having adopted its proposal. Because of the existing theological attitudes such a coming together of the two movements would lead to unhealthy confusion. Indeed, on the evangelical side it could mean a disastrous distortion of world mission today.

II. ON THE SIGNIFICANCE OF THE MANILA CONGRESS
A. A Good Continuation of Lausanne I

Taken as a whole we find the course and the results of the Second International Congress for World Evangelization to be a cause for great thanksgiving. The "Manila Manifesto" provides hope for us that the evangelical movement will remain true to its stated programme in the "Lausanne Commitment" of 1974. We welcome especially the following aspects of the Manila Congress:

1. Lausanne II upheld with the utmost clarity the biblically-revealed uniqueness of Jesus Christ as the only way to God the Father for all mankind. Thus the Geneva understanding of mission and dialogue was clearly rejected.

2. The assembly emphasised strongly the urgency of witnessing to Christ among people who have not yet been reached with the gospel. In keeping with the Lausanne Covenant § 6, the assembly thus held firmly to the priority of proclamation in the overall task of mission.

3. Underscored at the same time was the special responsibility of Christian witnesses toward the physical and social needs of the recipients of the message. The millions of handicapped persons were identified as a frequently overlooked mission-field.

4. The Church of Jesus Christ as a whole was viewed as the mediator of the evangelistic witness, and the responsibility of the local congregation was emphasised.

5. More clearly than in earlier times the Lausanne Movement in Manila took its stand with brothers and sisters suffering persecution for Jesus' sake.

6. The Lausanne Executive Committee, following the appeal from Os Guinness, adopted the slogan "Mission in the modern

world without worldliness in mission" to express the central challenge of the years to come.

B. Weaknesses Appearing at the Congress

Despite our appreciation of Lausanne II in Manila we do not overlook the theological vagueness which the Congress occasionally showed. In particular the following questions were not satisfactorily answered:

1. Does the biblical order of things, with its greater emphasis on salvation than on physical well-being (Mk. 1:34-38; 2:5) remain intact if, in the framework of Manila's "integrated" understanding of mission, the physical need of the person carries the same weight as his/her spiritual need?

2. Which theological understanding of "the poor" is presupposed, where the poor are especially declared to be the recipients of the message about Christ? What constitutes that poverty which the Bible addresses?

3. What theological understanding of "fulness of the Spirit" applies when this appears as the prerequisite for empowered evangelism? Moreover, what is the relationship of "signs and wonders" to the missionary message, when the Scriptures often associate these with the deception which will occur in the last days (Mt. 24:24; 2 Thess. 2:4f; Rev 13:13)?

4. What is the relationship between the Kingdom of God, in its present and future form, and the Church of Jesus Christ?

5. By what right does the Congress apply the term "incarnational"—a term which stems from the doctrine of the Son of God becoming flesh—to the requirement for mission to adapt itself to the social and cultural environment?

6. In the perspective of the Bible and of the Reformation, what interpretation do the non-Christian religions receive, particularly as touching their demonic side (1 Cor. 10:20f; 2 Cor. 6:14-16)—an aspect which is frequently overlooked?

7. What is the significance of biblical eschatological prophecy for the orientation and form of evangelism? It is precisely at this

point that the Congress fell short of giving full answer to the theme which it set for itself, "Proclaim Christ until he comes!"

C. Signs of Threatening Influences

Along with a certain theological weakness the Manila Congress also brought to light some alien influences affecting the Lausanne Movement. These could, if they remain unchecked, pose a serious threat to the further course of the Movement as a healthful institution. There are in particular three sources of danger which we see here:

1. The first is the steady advance of the "Charismatic Movement," which sees itself as a spiritual renewal movement. Especially in its "third wave" does it lay claim to being the decisive force for the renewal of Christendom as a whole, and as an eschatological empowering for its mission. Apart from this rather presumptuous self-assessment in comparison with other renewal movements and traditions, the Charismatic Movement directly endangers the biblical understanding of mission. For there is a shift here in the central proclamation, away from Christ Crucified (1 Cor. 1:22-23; 2:2) toward the manifestations and gifts of the Holy Spirit. This leads to a certain loss of spiritual reality and balance. The practical danger to mission begins where, with this new quest for the Spirit—who according to the Johannine witness is the Spirit of truth (Jn. 14:17; 15:20)—there is no consequential enquiry into biblical truth and sound doctrine (1 Tim. 1:3; 4:1, 16), nor a compliance with the command to discern the spirits (2 Cor. 11:4; 1 Jn. 4:1-6).

2. Second, and of equal note, is the no less determined effort of the so-called "radical evangelicals" to set up a "Kingdom Theology," which arises out of an "integrated" understanding of salvation and mission (see above, II.B.1). Dangerous here is the levelling-out of the divinely-ordained eras in salvation history which have to do with the final realization of God's saving purpose. For the most passionate advocates of this theology the corresponding view of mission is very close to that of the social revolutionaries in

the Geneva Ecumenical Movement. This further encourages attempts at "bridge-building."

3. Finally, questionable influences are also present where individuals and organizations attempt to calculate and contrive in advance their missionary results according to their own set goals ("AD 2000"). They rely on carefully calculated statistics and the use of modern strategies and technologies. What is dangerous here is an excessive trust in the human ability to achieve something which God alone can grant, and a resulting perversion of God's mission into a human mission.

III. TOWARDS A BIBLICAL "HEILSGESCHICHTLICH" VIEW OF MISSION

Our position as so far explained has shown, on the one hand, our concern for the direction of the Geneva Division of Missions, in which it has calmly estranged itself from the biblical view by locking mission into a "here and now" exhibition of salvation and unity. On the other hand, regarding the Lausanne Movement, we have expressed our appreciation, while at the same time addressing the theological weaknesses and external influences which could endanger its scriptural basis.

Therefore, the future of efforts toward international mission appears promising to us only in so far as both streams, by rejecting any anti-biblical spirit and resisting all alien influences, come to a renewed and deepened consciousness of the biblical "heilsgeschichtlich" view of mission. This present statement is to be understood as an earnest call to such a consciousness, in thankful indebtedness to a heritage which was grounded in the missiology of the Reformation and of classical Pietism. We are reminded of the fact that representatives of this heritage—men such as Karl Heim, Karl Hartenstein and Walter Freytag—once desired to integrate this heritage in a helpful and corrective way into the ecumenical theology of mission. In the present discussion about the commission of the Church of Jesus Christ in this world there are above all ten key affirmations concerning the biblical "heilsgeschichtlich" thought about mission, which appear to us to be crucial:

1. The Source, Content and Goal of Mission

Mission arises out of the biblically-revealed plan of salvation of the Triune God (Jn. 3:16; Eph. 1:9-10; 1 Tim. 2:4), and proclaims the good news that God was in Christ reconciling the world to himself (2 Cor. 5:19-21). Through this established work of reconciliation people are rescued out of their sinful and lost condition, brought under the merciful rule of Christ (Col. 1:12-14; 1 Pet. 2:9), and prepared for the coming glorious Kingdom of God (Mt. 25:34; 1 Cor. 15:24-28). The ultimate goal is "that God may be all in all." Mission, then, is to concern itself, first and last, with giving glory to the holy God!

2. Mission's Message of Hope

Mission addresses a message of true hope to a humanity which has fallen prey to spiritual ruin and, as a result, is also increasingly threatened by external disaster (Acts 2:40; Gal. 3:15; Eph. 2:1ff; 1 Tim. 4:10; Tit. 1:2). The "poor in spirit," that is, those who realize their full helplessness and humbly acknowledge that they can make no demands upon God (Mt. 5:3; Isa. 57:15), are the ones who accept the gospel and experience its joy. Having been reconciled to God through Christ, our persistent trust in Him allows us to bear patiently the sufferings of the present age (Rom. 5:1-5; 8:17-25) and encourages us at the same time to alleviate or to prevent the suffering of our fellow human beings (Lu. 12:35-48; Gal. 6:9f; Jas. 2:14-17).

3. The Empowering for Mission

Mission is only possible through reliance upon the personal presence of the exalted Son of God, promised to his messengers (Mt. 28:20), and upon the help of the Holy Spirit, who is responsible for the effective delivery of the message (Jn. 16:8-11; Acts 1:8). Since the task of mission can only be accomplished in the closest possible fellowship with the Triune God, a firm steadfastness in Him and in His Word and Sacrament (Jn. 6:53-58; 15:1-8; 1 Cor. 11:26) is the basic prerequisite for all missionary activity. In addition to this the prayers of the missionary church are extremely important (Eph. 6:18-20).

4. The Battlefield of Mission

Just as the Son of God came into the world to free it from its demonic occupying forces through His own obedience unto death (Jn. 12:31; 1 Jn. 3:8b), so also does Jesus send His disciples (Jn. 20:21) into the world as sheep among wolves (Mt. 10:1, 16). Christian mission bears in mind the fact that the people of this fallen world, in every area of their lives, their religions and their cultures, all stand within the devil's sphere of influence (Lu. 4:6; Jn. 14:30; 1 Cor. 4:4; Eph. 2:2; Rev. 12:9). Only by accepting for themselves the victory won at Golgotha (Rev. 12:11) is it possible for those who come to faith to be saved from this perilous situation (Acts 14:15; Heb. 2:14). This missionary battle against the cunning spiritual powers of darkness must not be confused with political battles; it can only be fought with spiritual weapons (Eph. 6:10-18). Already during this period of evangelization the redemption of the world to its Creator is occurring by stages (Mt. 22:44; Lu. 10:18; Jn. 12:31; 1 Cor. 15:24-28; Rev. 12:8f), so that various cultures may enjoy its benefits (Phil. 4:8; Rev. 21:24). The ultimate overthrow of the devil will not, however, take place until the Lord returns with his heavenly host (Rev. 12:12; 19:11-20; 21:24). At that time the Lord will separate for ever the saved from the disobedient (Mt. 25:31-46).

5. Mission, the Holy Spirit, and the Discerning of Spirits

Mission follows the biblical admonition to discern the spirits (1 Jn. 4:1-3), for Satan is able to masquerade as an angel of light (2 Cor. 11:3-4, 14). The Holy Spirit does not seek personal glory, but rather glorifies Christ (Jn. 16:13f). With a positive watchfulness we must distinguish the Holy Spirit from the human spirit, as from all lying and deceitful spirits of demons (Acts 16:16-18), which, with all their many manifestations, are forerunners of the coming Antichrist (2 Thess. 2:7-12; 1 Jn. 4:3).

Since the Holy Spirit, by whom all born-again Christians are baptized into one body (1 Cor. 12:13), apportions gifts to each member of the body as He wills (v. 11), we have no right to strain after a supposed "fulness of the Spirit" which necessarily shows itself in the reappearance of all the early Christian miracles. The authorization which Jesus promised His disciples for their mission is much more to be seen in the continual assistance of the Holy Spirit. The Spirit will fill us and guide us (Gal. 5:18; Eph. 5:18), so as to lead us into all truth (Jn. 16:13; 14:26), and through our witness convict the world of sin, righteousness, and judgment to come (Jn. 16:7-11). To those authorized by Christ the Spirit gives power for the preaching of the Word, so that all who believe can make their own the priceless gift which Christ Himself purchased for us on the cross, namely the forgiveness of sins (Jn. 20:22f).

6. The Prospects for Mission

It is sufficient for the messengers of the Lord to know that while spiritual fruit is indeed promised for their faithful service there can be no guarantee of full success within the present order (Jn. 15:16). Rather we have to be prepared to meet increased spiritual struggles and persecutions as well as to suffer rejection (Mt. 10:16-25; Jn. 15:18-21). According to Jesus' prophecy, His return—which we are not able to calculate—will not be preceded by a Christianization of the world but by a great falling-away (Mt. 24:9-13). Therefore a readiness for sacrifice and martyrdom, together with an active brotherly sympathy for those who suffer because of their witness to Christ, will be positive proof of our own faithfulness (1 Pet. 5:8; Rev. 2:10; 12:11).

7. Church of Christ, Kingdom of God and Mission

By mediating the Lord's own Gospel of the Kingdom (Mk. 1:15) mission prepares the way for God's sovereign rule which He will set up when He returns in glory (Mt. 24:31). His church gathered together throughout the world represents the new humanity (Rom. 5:14; 2 Cor. 5:17f; Eph. 2:14-16) and constitutes already in this passing age the merciful dawning of that kingdom of Christ. As a truly alternative fellowship—that is, a fellowship which has been renewed by the Holy Spirit—the Church provides a foretaste of the coming kingdom of peace (Isa. 2:2-4) through its activity of love (Rom. 13:8-10; 2 Pet. 1:7) and justice. In this way, by the power of God's act of reconciliation in Christ, the church contributes to change in the world and in society from within (Mt. 13:33; Philemon; 1 Pet. 2:9f; Jas. 2:14-17).

8. The Temporary Nature of the Social Achievements of Mission

In respect of the role that we as Christians are commanded to fill in the bringing about of more human standards of living (Jer. 29:7; Mt. 5:13-16), mission soberly recognizes the limited and temporary nature of all efforts which have as their goal the preserving and reorganizing of conditions in the world (Mt. 26:11). Mission is aware of the inevitable end of the first creation, as a result of sin and the power of death which have invaded it (2 Pet. 3:7-10). The promise of a "holistic salvation" will not be realized until the future redemption of our bodies (Phil. 3:20f), in connection with the eschatological renewal of the entire creation which "groans until now" (Rom. 8:18-25). For this reason a "holistic salvation" cannot merely form the content of a "holistic programme of mission."

In the same way, the solidarity which mission ought to display with suffering humanity must not be allowed to lead us into involvement with selfish power-struggles. It is for this very reason that we are not able to call such solidarity "incarnational," for Christ's own incarnation took the exact opposite direction, namely the renunciation of power (Phil. 2:5-8)!

9. The Urgency of Mission

Mission is spurred on by a sense of holy urgency precisely because it awaits the complete fulfillment of the biblical promises of salvation at the return of Christ (Heb. 9:28b). Jesus linked his second coming, for the completion of his redemptive work, with a preceding testimony to his Gospel among all peoples, including Israel (Mt. 24:14; Acts 1:6-8; Rom. 11:25-27; 1 Cor. 9:16). At the same time mission is carried out in the awareness of the seasons of salvation history—"the times of the Gentiles" (Lu. 21:24b; Acts 16:9f)—which God has personally set for the proclamation of the Gospel and for its saving effects in those who receive it (Col. 3:1-4; 2 Pet. 3:9). At the time when the full number of the Gentiles have entered into salvation, then all Israel will be saved and God's purpose will have reached its triumphant goal (Rom. 11:11-15, 25-36).

10. The Confidence of Mission

Mission takes place in the joyful confidence that Jesus Christ, on the basis of the victory he has already won (Col. 2:15; Heb. 2:14-16) and of his approaching final victory at the Consummation (1 Cor. 15:25f; Rev. 19), will guide the work of his commissioned messengers step by step toward the fulfillment that God has prepared (Phil. 1:6). There is no human or superhuman adversary who can thwart this victory (Isa. 46:9f; 55:8-13; 1 Cor. 15:57f)!

THE OUTLOOK

We came together in Frankfurt at a time when striking events seem to be on the increase, not only in the political history of nations—as witness the break-up of the former "eastern Bloc"—but also in the natural order and in the life of the churches. The fact that at the same moment in Seoul, South Korea, the "World Convocation for Justice, Peace, and the Integrity of Creation" was meeting gave us pause for reflection. For at that conference the "Conciliar Process," given its initial impulse in Germany, attained for the first time a global ecumenical dimension. In our judgement the Conciliar Process presents a threat to the mission of the Church of Jesus Christ, in the form of a radical concentration on worldly issues which leads to a perversion of the Church's redemptive commission.

More important for us, however, was the gratifying news of

newly opening doors to areas in which the Gospel could not be freely proclaimed up to now.

Such a combination of circumstances at this time holds for us the force of a divine admonition, to respond all the more carefully and obediently to the great mandate of Jesus for mission and evangelism. Indeed, Jesus Himself urged us to discern the signs of the times (Mt. 24:32-33; Lu. 21:7-31). We are aware that only God the Father knows the final hour of history (Mk. 13:32); but we are commanded to be always ready (Lu. 12:39f) and to prove ourselves to be faithful servants in the carrying out of Christ's commission, calmly and soberly, until He comes again. Jesus Christ has promised, "Blessed is that servant whom his master when he comes will find so doing" (Lu. 12:43).

Therefore we unanimously uphold the theme of the Lausanne II Congress:

"Proclaim Christ until he comes!"

This statement was accepted unanimously by the participants of the European Convention of Confessing Fellowships and signed on behalf of the International Christian Network by The Rt. Rev. Oskar Sakrausky (Honorary President) and Professor Dr. Peter Beyerhaus (President).

SOURCES

*T*he first chapter is an abridged version of a paper delivered at the International Congress on World Evangelization, Lausanne II in Manila, July 19, 1989 under the original title: "Eschatology in Evangelism." Its full text appeared in *EMQ*, Fall 1990.

The second chapter is an edited version of a paper which was written in preparation for the International Congress on World Evangelization, Lausanne 1974. Its text appeared in the official reference volume *Let the Earth Hear His Voice*, J. D. Douglas, ed. (Minneapolis: World Wide Publications, 1975), pp. 283-295.

The third chapter is an edited version of a paper written in preparation for the Consultation on the Relation between Evangelism and Social Responsibility, Grand Rapids, Michigan, 1982, sponsored jointly by the Lausanne Committee on World Evangelization and the World Evangelical Fellowship. It appeared under the title "A Biblical Encounter with Some Contemporary Philosophical and Theological Systems" in the official reference volume *In Word and Deed*, Bruce Nicholls, ed. (Grand Rapids, MI: Eerdmans, 1985), pp. 165-187.

The fourth chapter is a reprint of a contribution to the book *God Who Is Rich in Mercy: Essays Presented to D. B. Knox*, P. T. O'Brien and D. G. Peterson, eds. (Homebush, West NSW, Australia: Anzea Publishers, 1986), pp. 153-183. The original title was:

"Blessed Are the Poor in Spirit. The Theology of the Poor in Biblical Perspective."

The fifth chapter is a translation of a section in my book *Aufbruch der Armen. Die neue Missionsbewegung nach Melbourne* (Verlag der Liebenzeller Mission, 1981), pp. 111-123.

The sixth chapter originally appeared as a separate booklet under the title *Theology as an Instrument of Liberation* (Cape Town: Pro Fide Defendenda, 1988).

The seventh chapter originally appeared as a separate booklet under the title *The Kairos Document—Challenge or Danger to the Church?* (Cape Town: Gospel Defence League, 1987). It was brought up to date for this new publication.

The eighth chapter is a translation of the concluding section of my book *Aufbruch der Armen* (Verlag der Liebenzeller Mission, 1981), pp. 223-226.

The ninth chapter is the adopted text of a paper delivered at the Jakunin Hearing, sponsored by Christian Solidarity International at the occasion of the Sixth General Assembly of the WCC in Vancouver on July 25, 1983. It appeared in German translation in *Orthodoxe Rundschau*, Special Issue 1984, under the title "*Die Bedeutung des Martyriums für den Aufbau des Leibes Christi.*"

The Appendix is a Declaration of the European Confession Congress, held at Frankfurt/Main on March 5-7, 1990. The draft and the final edition of the text was provided by the author; translation by Dennis Lindsay.

BIBLIOGRAPHY

MESSIANIC MARXISM

Bloch, Ernst, *Man on His Own* (New York: Herder & Herder, 1970).

———, *Atheismus im Christentum* (Frankfurt: a. M.: Suhrkamp, 1968).

Garaudy, Roger, *The Alternative Future: A Vision of Christian Marxism* (New York: Simon & Schuster, 1974).

———, *From Anathema to Dialogue* (New York: Vintage, 1966).

MARXIST-CHRISTIAN DIALOGUE

Aptheker, Herbert, *The Urgency of Marxist-Christian Dialogue* (New York: Harper & Row, 1970).

Klugmann, James, ed., *Dialogue of Christianity and Marxism* (London: Lawrence & Wishart, 1966).

Oestreicher, Paul, ed., *The Christian Marxist Dialogue* (New York: Macmillan, 1969).

THEOLOGIES OF HOPE, LIBERATION, ETC.

Alves, Rubém, *A Theology of Human Hope* (St. Meinrad, IN: Abbey, 1971).

Cox, Harvey, *The Feast of Fools* (New York: Harper & Row, 1969).

Gutiérrez, Gustavo, *A Theology of Liberation* (Maryknoll, NY: Orbis, 1973).

Moltmann, Jürgen, *Theology of Hope* (New York: Harper & Row, 1967).

Vree, Dale, *On Synthesizing Marxism and Christianity* (New York: John Wiley & Sons, 1976).

FUTUROLOGY

Hoke, Donald E., *Evangelicals Face the Future* (South Pasadena, CA: William Carey Library, 1978).

_____, *An Evangelical Agenda: 1984 and Beyond* (Pasadena, CA: William Carey Library, 1978).

Laszlo, Ervin, *Goals for Mankind* (London: Hutchinson Publishing Co., 1977).

Meadows, Dennis H., *Limits to Growth* (New York: University Books, 1972).

Mesarovic, Mihailo, *Mankind at the Turning Point* (New York: E. P. Dutton, 1974).

Tinbergen, Jan, *Reshaping the International Order* (New York: New American Library, 1976).

Toffler, Alvin, *Future Shock* (New York: Random, 1970; London: Pan Books, 1978).

ECUMENICAL UTOPIA

Beyerhaus, P./Betz, U., eds., *Ökumene im Spiegel von Nairobi* (Bad Liebenzell: Verlag der Liebenzeller Mission, 1976).

Lange, Ernst, *Die ökumenische Utopie* (Stuttgart: Kreuz-Verlag, 1972).

Lefever, Ernest W., *Amsterdam to Nairobi* (Washington, D.C.: Ethics and Public Policy Center, 1979).

Norman, Edward, *Christianity and the World Order* (New York: Oxford University Press, 1979).

Van der Bent, Ans, *The Utopia of World Community* (London: SCM Press, 1973).

SALVATION HISTORY

Conzelmann, Gerhard, *The Theology of St. Luke* (London/New York: Harper, 1960).
Cullmann, Oscar, *Heil als Geschichte* (Tübingen: Mohr, 1965).
Heim, Karl, *Jesus der Weltvollender* (Wuppertal: Aussaat, 1978).
———, *Weltschöpfung und Weltvollendung* (Wuppertal: Aussaat, 1977).
Von Rad, Gerhard, *The Message of the Prophets* (London: SCM Press, 1968).

NOTES

PREFACE

1. All three books were published by Zondervan Publishing House, Grand Rapids, MI.

CHAPTER ONE: *The Kingdom Vision in Evangelical Eschatology*

1. Dana L. Robert, "The Origin of the Student Volunteer Watchword: 'The Evangelization of the World in This Generation,'" in *International Bulletin of Missionary Research*, Vol. 10, No. 4 (October 1986), p. 147.
2. John R. Mott, in his Closing Address, delivered in the Assembly Hall at Edinburgh, June 23, 1910, in *The History and Records of the Conference: Official Report of the World Missionary Conference 1910*, Vol. IX (Edinburgh: Oliphant, Anderson, and Ferrier), p. 351.
3. Gustav Warneck, *Die moderne Weltevangelisationstheorie*, in *Allgemeine Missions-Zeitschrift*, Vol. 24 (1897), p. 305ff.
4. *The World Mission of the Church. Findings and Recommendations of the Meeting of the International Missionary Council*, Tambaram, Madras, India, December 12-29, 1938 (London/New York: International Missionary Council, 1939), p. 180f.
5. *Ibid.*
6. I have elaborated on the significance of the Uppsala Assembly in my book *Missions—Which Way? Humanization or Redemption* (Grand Rapids, MI: Zondervan, 1972).
7. Cf. my book *Bangkok '73—The Beginning or End of World Mission?* (Grand Rapids, MI: Zondervan, 1974).
8. Denton Lotz, *"The Evangelization of the World in this Generation": The Resurgence of a Missionary Idea Among the Conservative Evangelicals*, doctoral thesis, Hamburg, 1970, p. 231.

9. Documented in Harold Lindsell, ed., *The Church's World-Wide Mission* (Waco, TX: Word, 1966), pp. 217-237, especially p. 219.

10. Documented in Beyerhaus, *Missions—Which Way?*, pp. 107-120, especially pp. 118-120.

11. Basil Meeking and John Stott, eds., *The Evangelical—Roman-Catholic Dialogue on Mission 1977—1984* (Grand Rapids, MI: Eerdmans, 1986), p. 34f.

12. Documented in J. D. Douglas, ed., *Let the Earth Hear His Voice*, official reference volume (Lausanne, Switzerland: International Congress on World Evangelization, 1974), pp. 8-9 (para. 15).

13. Walter Freytag, "*Mission im Blick aufs Ende*," in *Reden und Aufsätze*, Part II (München: C. Kaiser, 1961), pp. 186-198.

14. David J. Hesselgrave, "The Millennium and Missions," in *EMQ*, Vol. 24 (1988), pp. 70-77.

15. I am aware that some premillennialists (in particular many of a dispensational orientation) understand Matt 24:14 and Mark 13:10 to speak of evangelism during a seven-year period of tribulation at the end of the present age. On the contrary, I maintain that these passages refer to evangelistic efforts that run the whole course of the age between Christ's first and second advents. For examples of dispensational interpretation of these passages, readers may consult such works as A. C. Gaebelein, *The Olivet Discourse: Matthew 24 & 25* (New York: Gospel Publishing House, n.d.); A. C. Gaebelein, *The Gospel of Matthew: An Exposition in Two Volumes*, Vol. 2 (Wheaton, IL: VanKampen Press, 1910), pp. 164-249; John R. Rice, *The King of the Jews: A Verse by Verse Commentary on the Gospel of Matthew* (Wheaton, IL: Sword of the Lord Publishers, 1955), pp. 366-399; and John F. Walvoord, *Matthew: Thy Kingdom Come* (Chicago: Moody Press, n.d.), pp. 179-204.

16. Oscar Cullmann, "*Eschatologie und Mission im Neuen Testament*" (1941), reprinted in K. Fröhlich, ed., *Oscar Cullmann—Vorträge and Aufsätze 1925-1962* (Tübingen: Mohr-Verlag, 1966), pp. 248-359.

17. M. W. Moorhead, ed., *The Student Missionary Enterprise* (Boston: Press of T. O. Metcalf and Co.,1894), p. 48.

18. Cf. P. Beyerhaus, "*Theologisches Verstehen nicht-christlicher Religionen*," in *Kerygma und Dogma*, Vol. 25 (1989), pp. 106-127.

19. Cf. Vonette Bright and Ben A. Jennings, eds., *Unleashing the Power of Prayer. Messages from the International Prayer Assembly* (Chicago: Moody Press, 1989).

CHAPTER TWO: *World Evangelization and the Kingdom of God*

1. Wilhelm Bousset, *Monographien über das Urchristentum—Jesu Predigt in ihrem Gegensatz zum Judentum* (Berlin: 1892), p. 23.

2. A. M. Hunter, *Introducing New Testament Theology* (London: SCM Press, 1957), pp. 34-36.

3. Rudolf Bultmann, *Theologie des Neuen Testaments* (Tübingen: Mohr-Verlag, 1953), p. 8f.

4. See footnote 9 in Chapter 1.

5. See footnote 10 in Chapter 1.

6. Some interpreters refer Matthew 24 and 25 to the seven-year period of tribulation at the end of the church age. Others believe they were fulfilled within the 1st century A.D. If one holds either of these views, he does not normally hold that world evangelization is the Church's contribution to establishing the Kingdom. For those who believe Matt 24:14 refers to the first century A.D., obviously that did not contribute to the establishment of the Kingdom. Even amillennialists who see the Kingdom present in this whole current age would hold that Christ himself established his Kingdom in the hearts of men at his first coming. Evangelism had nothing to do with it. Those who see Matt 24:14 as fulfilled during the seven-year tribulation at the end of the age would not normally see such evangelism as contributing to the establishing of the Kingdom. Christ himself will return at the end of the seven-year period of tribulation to destroy his enemies and establish the Kingdom. The timing is set by the seven-year duration of the tribulation, not by the amount of time it takes believers to evangelize the world during that tribulation. Though many have held such positions, my understanding of Matthew 24 is that it relates to the whole course of the Christian era and that the Church does play a significant role through evangelism in setting the stage for the inception of Christ's Kingdom.

CHAPTER THREE: *God's Kingdom and Modern Utopianism*

1. Erich Kellner, ed., *Christentum und Marxismus—heute: Gespräche der Paulus-Gesellschaft* (Wien: Europa-Verlag, 1966).

2. Gustavo Gutiérrez, *A Theology of Liberation* (Maryknoll, NY: Orbis, 1973); Andrew Kirk, *Liberation Theology. An Evangelical View from the Third World* (London: Marshall, Morgan & Scott, 1979).

3. Ernst Bloch, *Atheismus in Christendum* (Frankfurt am Main: Suhrkamp, 1968), S 350.

4. Ernst Bloch, *Das Prinzip Hoffnung*, 3 vols. (Berlin: Aufbau-Verlag, 1954-59).

5. Jürgen Moltmann, *Theology of Hope* (New York: Harper & Row, 1967).

6. Roger Garaudy, *The Alternative Future: A Vision of a Christian Marxism* (New York: Simon & Schuster, 1974).

7. To change the world and to change life.

8. Roger Garaudy, in *Marxisten und die Sache Jesu*, Iring Fetscher and Milan Machovec, eds. (Mainz: Kaiser, 1974), p. 28.

9. Ernst Bloch, *Works*, Volume V (Frankfurt a.M.: Suhrkamp, 1985), p. 1524.

10. Jürgen Moltmann, *Das Experiment Hoffnung* (München: Chr. Kaiser Verlag 1974), p. 50.

11. See Note 3.

12. Ernst Bloch, *Works*, Vol. III (Frankfurt a..M.: Suhrkamp, 1969), p. 335.

13. The pioneers of the school of materialistic exegesis are Fernando Belo, *Lecture matérialiste de l'évangile de Marc* (1974); Michel Clévenot, *Approaches matérialistes de la Bible* (Paris: Editions du Cerf, 1976); George

Casalis, *Les idées justes ne tombent pas du ciel* (Paris: Editions du Cerf, 1977); cf. P. Beyerhaus, *Aufbruch der Armen* (Bad Liebenzell: Verlag der Liebenzeller Mission, 1981), pp. 54-61.

14. Roger Garaudy, *Marxisten und die Sache Jesu*, p. 38.

15. Alvin Toffler, *Future Shock* (New York: Random, 1970; London: Pan Books, 1971).

16. The five volumes of the "Report to the Club of Rome" (1972-1977) are summarized by Donald E. Hoke in *Evangelicals Face the Future* (South Pasadena, CA: William Carey Library, 1978), pp. 3-8.

17. Charles Birch, "Creation, Technique and Survival of Mankind" (in German) in *Beiheft zur Ökumenischen Rundschau*, No. 30, p. 96; (in English in *Ecumenical Review*, January 1976).

18. Quoted in *Pembroke Observer*, September 8, 1980.

19. E. Ostermann, *Zukunft ohne Hoffnung?* (Neuhausen: Hänssler, 1975), p. 52.

20. Ervin Laszlo, "'Goals for Global Society. A Positive Approach to the Predicament of Mankind.' A Report to the Club of Rome. Project Description." Typescript November 1974. The title of the book published in 1977 is *Goals for Mankind* (New York: Dutton; London: Hutchinson Pub. Group).

21. Donald E. Hoke, *Evangelicals Face the Future*, p. 8.

22. J. A. E. Vermaat, in *Ökumene im Spiegel von Nairobi '75*, P. Beyerhaus/U. Betz, eds. (Bad Liebenzell: Verlag der Liebenzeller Mission, 1976), p. 213.

23. Quoted by Steven Paas, *Vrede en Eenheid in Europa* (Amsterdam: Bujten en Schipperheijn, 1973), p. 125.

24. Ernst Lange, *Die ökumenische Utopie oder: Was bewegt die Ökumenische Bewegung?* (Stuttgart: Kreuz Verlag, 1972).

25. M. M. Thomas, "Report of the Chairman of the Executive Committee," *Utrecht 1972* (Beiheft zur Ökumenischen Rundschau, No. 23), p. 16f. (in German).

26. Dale Vree, *On Synthesizing Marxism and Christianity* (New York: John Wiley & Sons, 1976).

27. P. Beyerhaus, *Aufbruch der Armen: Die neue Missionsbewegung nach Melbourne* (Bad Liebenzell: Verlag der Liebenzeller Mission, 1981).

28. *This Month*, No. 33, EPS (December 1972), p. 2f.

29. *Von Uppsala nach Nairobi*, epd-Dokumentation, Vol. 15 (Bielefeld: 1975), p. 205.

30. Philip Potter, "Report of the General Secretary," in *Breaking Barriers, Nairobi 1975*, David M. Paton, ed. (London/Grand Rapids, MI: SPCK/Eerdmans, 1976), p. 248.

31. M. M. Thomas, "Report of the Moderator of the Central Committee," in *ibid.*, p. 238.

32. Philip Potter, in *Evangelische Kommentare*, May 1976, pp. 277f.

33. *Ibid.* (see note 29), p. 254.

34. *Ibid.*

35. Karl Heim, *Weltschöpfung und Weltvollendung* (Wuppertal: Aussat, 1977).

36. Cf. the Manila Manifesto, in J. D. Douglas, ed., *Proclaim Christ Until He*

Comes. Lausanne II in Manila. International Congress on World Evangelization, 1989 (Minneapolis: World Wide Publications), p. 29.

CHAPTER FOUR: *The Kingdom—Christ's Promise to the Poor*

1. In the following I am indebted to Kuno Füssel, "*Materialistische Lektüre der Bibel, Bericht über einen alternativen Zugang zu biblischen Texten,*" in: Will: Schottroff/Wolfgang Stegemann, eds., *Der Gott der kleinen Leute. Sozialgeschichtliche Auslegungen,* Bd. I, *Altes Testament* (Munich: Kaiser/Burckhardthaus-Laetare, 1979), pp. 20-38.
2. *Your Kingdom Come. Mission Perspectives. Report on the World Conference on Mission and Evangelism, Melbourne, Australia, 12-25 May 1980* (Geneva: Commission on World Mission and Evangelism, World Council of Churches, 1980), p. 171.
3. *Ibid.,* p. 172.
4. Julia Esquivel, "The Crucified Lord: A Latin American Perspective," in *Your Kingdom Come,* pp. 52-60.
5. *Ibid.,* p. 55.
6. E. Bammel, "*ptōchos, ptōcheia, ptōcheuō,*" *TDNT* 6 (1968), p. 888.

CHAPTER FIVE: *The Ideological Transformation of the Kingdom at Melbourne 1980*

1. *Your Kingdom Come.* Preparatory Document for the CWME 1980 Conference (mimeographed), p. 1.
2. *Ibid.,* p. 13.
3. Jacques Matthey, ed., *Your Kingdom Come. Mission Perspectives. Report on the World Conference on Mission and Evangelism, Melbourne, Australia, May 12-26, 1980* (Geneva: World Council of Churches, 1980), p. 193.
4. *Your Kingdom Come.* Preparatory Document, p. 12.
5. Enrique Dussel, "The Kingdom of God and the Poor," *International Review of Mission (IRM),* Vol. LXVIII, No. 270 (April 1979), p. 125.
6. Oral information by a German participant to the author.
7. *Norsk Tidskrift for Misjon,* No. 1/1981, p. 3.
8. *Your Kingdom Come. Melbourne Report,* p. 183.
9. *Ibid.,* p. 187.
10. *Ibid.,* p. 188f.
11. Emilio Castro, "Your Kingdom Come: A Missionary Perspective," in *ibid.,* p. 30.
12. *Ibid.,* p. 31.
13. Metropolitan Geevarghese Mar Osthathios, "The Gospel of the Kingdom and the Crucified and Risen Lord," in *Your Kingdom Come. Melbourne Report,* p. 47.
14. *Ibid.,* p. 38.
15. Emilio Castro, Editorial to *IRM,* Vol. LXVIII, No. 270 (April 1979), p. 100.
16. Enrique Dussel, "The Kingdom of God and the Poor," in *ibid,* p. 125.
17. *Ibid.,* p. 48.

CHAPTER SIX: *People's Theologies in Quest for a Political Kingdom*

1. *Herausgefordert durch die Armen: Dokumente der Ökumenischen Vereinigung von Dritte-Welt-Theologen 1976-1983*, Ludwig Wiedenmann, ed. (Feiburg: Herder, 1983), p. 10.

2. "Die Kirchen in der Dritten Welt und ihre theologische Aufsabe," in: *Ökumenische Rundschau* (German edition of *Ecumenical Review*) (February 1977), p. 211.

3. Philip Potter, "Doing Theology in a Divided World," *Ecumenical Review* (July 1983), p. 208f.

4. Resolutions of Commission, at the First Latin American meeting of "Christians for Socialism," in Santiago, Chile, published in *Los Cristianos por el Socialismo* (Siglo Veintinno, Argentina: 1977). Quoted by Bonaventura Kloppenburg, *Die Neue Volkskirche* (Aschaffenburg: Pattlach Verlag, 1981), p. 20.

5. Hans-Martin Moderow and Matthias Sens, eds., *Orientierung Ökumene: Ein Handbuch Evangelische Verlag Sanstalt* (Berlin: Evangelische Verlagsanstalt, 1979), p. 79f.

6. Cf. Peter Beyerhaus, *Aufbruch der Armen* (Bad Liebenzell: Verlag der Liebenzeller Mission, 1981), p. 32f.

7. Cf. Åge Holter, *Norsk Tidskift for Misjon* (March 1978), p. 152ff.

8. Emilio Castro, *International Review of Mission* (October 1977), p. 311ff.

9. *Ökumenische Rundschau* (February 1977), p. 221ff.

10. M. M. Thomas, *Bericht aus Nairobi 75* (Geneva: ÖRK [World Council of Churches], 1976), p. 246.

11. *Ökumenische Rundschau* (February 1977), p. 221.

12. Bonaventura Kloppenburg, *Die Neue Volkskirche* (Aschaffenburg, 1981), p. 67.

13. *Ökumenische Rundschau* (February 1979), p. 139.

14. Teresa Dagdag, "Towards the Emergence of a People's Theology in the Philippines," *Ching Feng* (September 1982), p. 139f.

15. Wiedenmann, ed., *Herausgefordert durch die Armen: Dokumente der Ökumenischen Vereinigung von Dritte-Welt-Theologen 1976-1983*, p. 124.

16. *Ibid.*, p. 79.

17. Bonaventura Kloppenburg, *Die Neue Volkskirche*, p. 51.

18. Dagdag, "Towards the Emergence of a People's Theology in the Philippines," p. 146.

19. Wiedenmann, ed., *Herausgefordert durch die Armen: Dokumente der Ökumenischen Vereinigung von Dritte-Welt-Theologen 1976-1983*, p. 130.

20. *Ibid.*, p. 131.

21. Cited in Bonaventura Kloppenburg, *Die Neue Volkskirche*, p. 81.

22. Teresa Dagdag, "Towards the Emergence of a People's Theology in the Philippines," p. 144.

23. *Ökumenische Rundschau* (February 1977), p. 215.

24. Philip Potter, "Doing Theology in a Divided World," p. 28.

25. Cf. Peter Beyerhaus, *Aufbruch der Armen*, p. 39ff.

26. Severino Croatto, "*Befreiung und Freiheit. Biblische Hermeneutic für die Theologie der Befreiung*," in *Theologie der Dritten Welt* (Hamburg: EMW, 1979).

27. Julia Esquivel, "The Crucified Lord: A Latin American Perspective," in *Your Kingdom Come, Report on the World Conference on Mission and Evangelism* (Geneva: World Council of Churches, 1980), p. 54.

28. Cf. Kuno Füssel, "*Materialistische Lektüre der Bibel*," in *Der Gott der kleinen Leute*, W. Schrottroff and W. Stegemann, eds., Vol. 1, p. 20f.; and George Casalis, *Die richtigen Ideen fallen nicht vom Himmel* (Kohlhammer-Verlag, 1979).

29. Ahn Byung Mu, "*Was ist Minjung-Theologie? Zur 'Theologies des Volkes' in Südkorea*," *Junge Kirche* (June 1982), p. 209ff.

30. Cited by Bonaventura Kloppenburg, *Die Neue Volkskirche*, p. 79.

31. *Ibid.*, p. 80.

32. *Ibid.*

33. My own report of Dorothee Sölle's lecture "Theology in the 80s" at the WCC Conference in Vancouver 1983.

34. Cf. M. M. Thomas, *Bericht aus Nairobi*, p. 132.

35. Julia Esquivel, "The Crucified Lord: A Latin American Perspective," p. 54.

36. Byung Mu Ahn, "*Was ist Minjung-Theologie? Zur 'Theologies des Volkes' in Südkorea*," p. 295f.

37. Raimond Fung, "Good News for the Poor—Its Implications for a Missionary Movement," in *Your Kingdom Come, Report on the World Conference on Mission and Evangelism* (Geneva: World Council of Churches, 1980), p. 146f.

38. Teresa Dagdag, "Towards the Emergence of a People's Theology in the Philippines," p. 146f.

39. Byung Mu Ahn, "*Was ist Minjung-Theologie? Zur 'Theologie des Volkes' in Südkorea*," p. 295.

40. G. Mar Osthathios, "*Das Evangelium vom Reich Gottes und dem gekreustigten und auferstandenen Herrn*," in *Dein Reich komme. Bericht der Weltkonferenz für Mission und Evangelisation in Melbourne 1980* (Frankfurt a. M.: 1980), p. 104.

41. Byung Mu Ahn, "*Was ist Minjung-Theologie? Zur 'Theologies des Volkes' in Südkorea*," p. 296.

42. *Ibid.*, p. 292.

43. *Ibid.*

44. *Ökumenische Rundschau* (February 1977), p. 211.

45. *Ibid.*, p. 220.

46. Teresa Dagdag, "Towards the Emergence of a People's Theology in the Philippines," p. 147.

47. Bonaventura Kloppenburg, *Die Neue Volkskirche*, p. 61.

48. Trutz Rendtorff, "*Universalität und Kontextualität der Theologie*," ZThK (1977).

49. V. Fabella and S. Torres, *Irruption of the Third World—A Challenge to Christian Theology* (New York: Maryknoll, 1983).

50. *Ökumenische Rundschau* (February 1977), p. 211.

CHAPTER SEVEN: *What Kingdom Is at Hand?*

1. I am using and quoting from the German edition in *Christliches Bekenntnis in Südafrika*, 2nd edition, Evangelisches Missionswerk, ed. (Hamburg: Das Kairos Dokument. Herausforderung an die Kirche, 1987), pp. 3-39.
2. Mimeographed text, attainable from the Rhenish Evangelical Church's head office at Düsseldorf, West Germany.
3. German translation in the same publication as footnote 1, pp. 56-88.
4. German translation in EMW-Informationen No.82, Hamburg 1988.
5. *The Road to Damascus. Kairos and Conversion* (Johannesburg: Skotaville Publishers; copyright by Institute of Contextual Theology, 1989).
6. Cf. previous chapter.
7. Cf. previous chapter, footnote 27.
8. KD, chapter 1, *loc.cit.*, p. 9.
9. Sunand Sumithra, *Revolution as Revelation. A Study of M.M. Thomas's Theology* (Tübingen/New Delhi: International Christian Network/ Theological Research and Communications Institute, 1984).
10. According to the Information Service of the German Evangelical Alliance *idea*, No. 20/90, March 7, 1990, p. 4.
11. Cf. Hans Steubing, ed., *Bekenntnisse der Kirche* (Wuppertal: Theologischer Verlag R. Brockhaus, 1977), pp. 287-289.
12. *Loc.cit.* (see footnote 1), p. 15.
13. Cf. previous chapter.
14. *Loc.cit.*, p. 18.
15. *Ibid.*, p. 7.
16. For a deeper unfolding of this thought I highly recommend the autobiographical book of my friend Michael Cassidy, *The Passing Summer. A South African Pilgrimage in the Politics of Love* (Kent, GNG: Dunton, Green, SevenOaks, 1989).

CHAPTER NINE: *Martyrdom—Gate to the Kingdom of Heaven*

1. Augustinus, *De civitate Dei*, Lib. XVIII, Cap. LI, 2 *migne, patres latini*, Series I, Vol. XLI, p. 614.
2. K. Marx in the Preface to his doctoral thesis, "*Uber die Differenz der demokritischen und epikureischen Naturphilosophie,*" in: *K. Marx, Frühe Schriften*, Vol. I, H. J. Lieber, ed. (Darmstadt: 1962), p. 21f.
3. Quoted by Richard Wurmbrand, *Marx and Satan* (Wheaton, IL: Crossway Books, 1986), p. 59.
4. Arthur Reynolds, *Pathway to Glory* (London: Overseas Missionary Fellowship, 1968), quoted from the German edition (Giessen, 1969), p. 17.
5. *Samizdat: Chronik eines neuen Lebens in der Sowjetuion*, ed. *pro fratribus* (Jesuitenplatz 4, Koblenz, 1975), p. 31.
6. *Ibid.*, p. 195.
7. *Ibid.*, p. 237.
8. Very vague references are made to this incident in the Official Report of the

Fifth Assembly of the WCC, *Breaking Barriers. Nairobi 1975*, David M. Paton, ed. (Grand Rapids, MI: Eerdmans, 1976), pp. 169-172.

APPENDIX: World Missions Following San Antonio and Manila 1989

1. As the conference moderator, he gave a keynote address in San Antonio—which unfortunately was hardly discussed by the Conference—printed in the *Conference Report: International Review of Mission*, Vol. LXVIII, Nos. 311/312 (July/October 1989), pp. 311-328.
2. Cf. the papers by Dr. E. Stockwell ("Mission Issues for Today and Tomorrow," *ibid*., pp. 303-315) and Ch. Duraisingh ("San Antonio and Some Continuing Concern of the CWMA," *ibid*., pp. 400-408).
3. E. Stockwell, *ibid*., p. 343.
4. *Ibid*., p. 357.
5. *Ibid*., p. 365.
6. *Ibid*., p. 356. Cf. P. Beyerhaus/L. E. V. Padberg eds., *Der konziliare Prozess—Realität and Utopie* (Asslar 1990.)
7. *IRM* (July/October 1982), pp. 431-435.

SCRIPTURE INDEX

GENERAL INDEX